EDINBURGH PEOPLE

AT WORK AND LEISURE

Finale at the Edinburgh Military Tattoo on the Castle esplanade, *c.*1950. *Photograph by Norward Inglis.*

PICTORIAL
EDINBURGH
SERIES

Malcolm Cant

EDINBURGH PEOPLE

AT WORK AND LEISURE

MALCOLM CANT
PUBLICATIONS

To
Naomi
my sixth granddaughter
'Just something to take home'

First published in 2006 by
Malcolm Cant Publications
13 Greenbank Row
Edinburgh EH10 5SY

ISBN 10: 0 9526099 9 1
ISBN 13: 978 0 9526099 9 5

British Library Cataloguing-in-Publication Data

A catalogue record for this book is available on request

Book and cover design by Mark Blackadder

Printed and bound by
The Cromwell Press,
Trowbridge, Wiltshire, UK

CONTENTS

BY THE SAME AUTHOR

Marchmont in Edinburgh 1984

Villages of Edinburgh Volume 1 (North) 1986

Villages of Edinburgh Volume 2 (South) 1987

Edinburgh: Sciennes and the Grange 1990

Yerbury: A Photographic Collection 1850-1993 1994

Edinburgh: Gorgie and Dalry 1995

Villages of Edinburgh: An Illustrated Guide Volume 1 (North) 1997

The District of Greenbank in Edinburgh 1998

Villages of Edinburgh: An Illustrated Guide Volume 2 (South) 1999

Old Tollcross, Morningside and Swanston 2001

Marchmont, Sciennes and the Grange 2001

Old Dalry in Edinburgh 2002

Old Gorgie 2002

Edinburgh from the Air: 70 Years of Aerial Photography 2003

Old Dean and Stockbridge 2004

Knowing Your Grandfather 2004

Edinburgh Shops Past and Present 2005

INTRODUCTION AND ACKNOWLEDGEMENTS

The *Pictorial Edinburgh Series*, which began in 2005 with *Edinburgh Shops Past and Present*, is basically a photographic record of various aspects of the City which are in danger of being lost from the public domain. Many of the photographs included are from family albums, but as time goes by the identity of the people in the photographs is known by a smaller and smaller group of people. Although it is simply not possible to trace and record everything, provided a reasonable number is kept, future generations will be able to see how ordinary people lived, dressed, worked and relaxed. The chronological spread is from the late nineteenth century to the present day.

The book is divided into three parts, between which are two colour sections. Part 1 is devoted to children and families, starting with infants in prams and moving through the full spectrum of family life. Part 2 deals with leisure activities and attendance at school and church. Although the activities are quite familiar, even to present-day youngsters, it has to be said that the design and quality of the school equipment, sports gear, bicycles and fairground attractions are infinitely better nowadays. What has not changed, of course, are the expressions of delight, apprehension and even boredom on the faces of the many children photographed. The church-related pictures are equally interesting, particularly the safety precautions, or lack of them, deemed necessary for Sunday School picnics. Part 3 deals with aspects of work and various groups on parade. Many of the occupations included are as relevant today as they were when the photographs were taken but there are important differences. Many jobs were gender-orientated and a high proportion of the staff lived within walking distance of their place of work. Nowadays the transport sector is as important as ever it was but bears little resemblance to the Dodge taxis, steam-driven vehicles and electric trams seen in the photographs. In the fire, police, ambulance and hospital section, every fire station and every hospital photographed has now been closed. The last photograph in the book shows the Royal Scots marching into the history books as an independent regiment.

It is not possible to put together a book of this nature without the assistance of several people. This is particularly the case in locating a sufficient number of photographs to make the book worthwhile. I was greatly assisted in the early stages of research by Barbara Simpson, whose father, Norward Inglis, had taken many photographs of Edinburgh, especially in the 1950s. Some of his work appears throughout the book. Other collectors of Edinburgh material also lent photographs from their own archive, including: Alan Brotchie; Elizabeth Casciani; Colin Dale; Louise Jenkins; Pat and Douglas Scoular; and the daughter of Frank Wilson. In addition to the collectors, many people allowed me to reproduce material from their family albums. Their names appear below the respective photographs throughout the book. Other people assisted me with general information. In alphabetical order they are: Joan Bakewell; Mrs Kerry Barker; Hamish Coghill; Val Dean; Sir Tom Farmer; Lyn Irvine; Margaret McArthur; Mrs Freda McIntyre; Roddy Martine; Sandy Mullay; Cardinal Cormac Murphy-O'Connor; Cardinal Keith O'Brien; Helen and Bill Teviotdale; David Valentine and Arthur Wood. The colour sections of the book contain a mixture of traditional and modern photography. The modern pictures are the work of Bryan Montgomery, Peter Stubbs, Phyllis M. Cant and Jenni Wood.

I also relied on assistance from various libraries and national archives, including: CHILDREN 1ST; the Court of the Lord Lyon; Cramond Heritage Trust; Edinburgh Room of the Central Library; Faculty of Advocates; *Gorgie Dalry Gazette*; Lothian & Borders Fire Brigade; Lothian & Borders Police Information Office; National Library of Scotland; National Museums of Scotland; Newhaven Heritage Centre; Royal College of Nursing Archives; Scotsman Publications Ltd; and Simmons Aerofilms Ltd.

After I had finished writing the book the serious business of publication began: Kate Blackadder edited the script to a very high standard; Mark Blackadder brought the basic material to life with his page and cover design; and Oula Jones completed a very comprehensive index. Without the commitment of those professional people I would not be able to publish my own books.

As always, I thank my wife Phyllis and the members of our ever-increasing extended family for their interest and assistance with numerous tasks.

Malcolm Cant
2006

PART 1: CHILDREN AND FAMILIES

Part 1 has 66 photographs of children and families from many parts of the City, the earliest of which is dated *c.* 1891. Being able to date and name the people in the photographs is of great importance to the researcher as it helps to explain some of the social conventions of the day, i.e. the style of clothes, the type of toys and even the choice of names. Families were, of course, much bigger in the earlier days and often lived in quite small houses by modern standards, like the Hastie family at Kirkgate who appear on this page. It was a great social event for members of a whole family to dress in their best clothes and go to one of the many portrait photographers to be recorded for posterity.

Part 1 begins with a double-page spread illustrating the many styles of prams used by mothers and nannies, including smaller versions used by the girls for their favourite dolls. There are also several photographs of children playing in the street and even posing for a photograph in the middle of the roadway. The back-green area of Edinburgh's

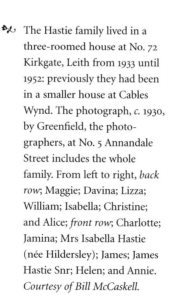 The Hastie family lived in a three-roomed house at No. 72 Kirkgate, Leith from 1933 until 1952: previously they had been in a smaller house at Cables Wynd. The photograph, *c.* 1930, by Greenfield, the photographers, at No. 5 Annandale Street includes the whole family. From left to right, *back row*; Maggie; Davina; Lizza; William; Isabella; Christine; and Alice; *front row*; Charlotte; Jamina; Mrs Isabella Hastie (née Hildersley); James; James Hastie Snr; Helen; and Annie. *Courtesy of Bill McCaskell.*

many tenement districts was also one of the most popular venues, often with the washing and the clothes poles acting as extra props. Other locations included various public parks such as Hillend, Colinton Dell, Blackford Pond and Starbank Park at Newhaven with its ornate, working fountain, or even the family allotment which has maintained its popularity to the present day. Some children were also fortunate to be photographed with leading show-biz personalities of the day as with Neill Boyd sitting with Jack Milroy on the day of a charity match at the Carlton Cricket Club in Grange Loan.

On 2 June 1953, Edinburgh, in common with the rest of the country, held street parties on Coronation Day. Although the weather was not good, most areas of the City organised events for the children. Home-made hats, home-baking and chairs borrowed from the local church hall were the order of the day.

The social conditions in which the children were reared are also evident in some of the photographs. Hand-me-down boots and shoes, and jackets with buttons and hems still pertaining to the previous incumbent were all part of the overall picture. Particularly poignant is the group of well-dressed and cared for children photographed at the Children's Shelter in New Assembly Close in

the High Street. A few pages have also been devoted to the children and families of what would probably nowadays be referred to as captains of industry. As befits their social status at the time, their houses are grander and many of the photographs include the children's nannies and other staff.

In some of the photographs towards the end of Part 1, the adults appear, particularly young mothers proudly holding their young offspring. The absence of the fathers in this type of picture might be explained by the fact that they took the picture. There is also a short section on wedding groups in 1927, 1934 and 1955. By nowadays standards, the photographs all appear to be excessively formal but are certainly a tribute to the photographer's power of persuasion to cajole the grooms into adopting such unfamiliar poses.

Occasionally the same person appears in photographs taken at different times in their life. Of particular interest is Alexander Dobson who appears on page 71 (Part 3) as a young slater working on the construction of the Edinburgh City Poorhouse at Glenlockhart, and in Part 1 on the day of his fortieth wedding anniversary. Another example is young Nell Hannah who appears, as a child, fishing in the Water of Leith in Colinton Dell and then, as an adult, holding her own child at Bruce Street in Morningside.

The McLennan family at No. 16 Dalziel Place, Abbeyhill, *c.* 1909. From left to right, *back row*; William Jnr; William Snr; *middle row*, Charlie; James; Mrs Jean McLennan (née Hamilton); David; *front row*, Margaret; and Dinah. *Courtesy of Jean McCaskell.*

Right. Twins, Margaret and Douglas Scoular, born 28 July 1937, photographed near Baird Avenue, *c.* 1938. When the photograph was taken, the twins lived with their mother and father, Archibald and Jemima Scoular in the family home on the top floor of No. 81 Gorgie Road. Twins had not been expected, which meant that the delighted parents had to make a hurried, return visit to Borthwick's pram shop in Cockburn Street to have a second hood fitted. The chassis-built pram had three removable boards which could be repositioned, either to accommodate the children as they grew bigger, or for storage, especially for going the messages. *Courtesy of Douglas Scoular.*

Below right. This undated photograph shows a delightful family group, all in their Sunday best, outside their main-door flat, No. 2, at the west end of Hermitage Park, off Lochend Road. *Malcolm Cant Collection.*

Below. Mother and family at Blackford Pond in the early part of the twentieth century at a time when the surrounding vegetation, and that on the lower slopes of Blackford Hill, was much lighter than at the present day. The pond-keeper's hut is at the far end, behind which are the terraced houses of Charterhall Road. Blackford Hill was acquired from Lt. Col. Henry Trotter of Mortonhall in 1884 for the sum of £8,000. Ian Nimmo records in *Edinburgh's Green Heritage* that the area around the Pond, previously known as Egyptfield, was not acquired until 1906. *Malcolm Cant Collection.*

❧ *Left.* The Penman family later of Craigview, Marchhall Road with their nursemaid, *c.* 1891. From left to right: Gertrude Margaret (Gerty); nurse 'Hattie'; Olive; Nell (being held by nurse 'Hattie'); Alice Jane (Dolly); and John Edgar (Jack). Further details of the Penman family appear on pages 16 and 17. *Courtesy of Miss Constance MacKenzie.*

❧ *Below left.* Mary McPhie, aged four, of No. 232 Easter Road, was required to adopt a studio pram and doll, rather than her own, for the purpose of this photograph by Jeromes of Leith Walk in 1930.
Courtesy of Mrs Mary Burnie, née McPhie.

❧ *Below centre.* Douglas and Dorothy Napier with their mother, Gertrude, at the small pedestrian bridge over the Braid Burn, with the hay ricks of Greenbank Farm in the background, *c.* 1924. *Courtesy of Mrs Jean Napier.*

❧ *Below.* Annot Moonie with her doll and pram on the Links pathway beside Warrender Park Terrace in 1932. At the time, Annot was living with her parents, Janet and William, and her brother, Graham, at the family home at No. 4 Strathfillan Road. *Courtesy of Graham Moonie.*

Right. One sock up and one sock down; a suspicious sheen on his left cuff; and a strategically placed button completes the picture of sartorial elegance for Jimmy Nisbet in the centre of the picture, flanked by his older brother, Willie, on the left, and their best pal, Jackie Boyd, on the right. The photograph was taken outside No. 14 Wardlaw Place in 1931. A little more than a decade after this photograph was taken Jackie Boyd was a fighter pilot during the Second World War and Willie Nisbet was sailing with the Royal Navy. *Courtesy of Jack Boyd.*

Below. A group of girls and boys in the back green of No. 16 Wardlaw Place in 1933. More than seventy years after the photograph was taken, four of the group can still be identified: *back row*, left, Walter Darling; *back row*, right, James Dobie; *front row*, first from the left, Jimmy Nisbet; *front row*, second from the left, Jackie Boyd. *Courtesy of Jack Boyd.*

❧ *Top left.* In 1935 Morningside was fortunate to have its own infantry. A contingent is seen here, at attention, in the back green of No. 49 Falcon Gardens. From left to right: Graham Moonie; his sister Annot Moonie; Myles Crooke; and Dougie.

❧ *Below left.* Still on parade, and at the ready, the contingent moves off, minus Annot, but under the watchful eye of Marjorie Murray.

❧ *Above.* This early twentieth-century photograph shows Falcon Road, looking east towards the south, or lower, end of Falcon Gardens. No. 49, already referred to, is the main door house facing towards the camera.

❧ *Below.* In 1938 the Falcon area was by no means fully built up. On the right of the picture, flats are under construction in Falcon Road West and the area of present-day Falcon Court is still open ground.
All courtesy of Graham Moonie.

❧ *Above.* A street photographer of the 1930s catches two distinct groups: on the left, the intended subjects for a possible sale; and, on the right, a group of local children, at least one of whom is aware of the camera. The photograph was taken in Gorgie Road, with the brick-built houses of White Park behind the van. *Malcolm Cant Collection.*

❧ *Right.* A young girl reaches the safety of the pavement in Blackfriars Street in the 1950s. Motorised transport is almost non-existent and the street is still lit by bracket lamps attached to the front of the tenements. On the right of the picture there is a sign 'Provisions, Confectionery' on a tenement which was demolished many years ago and subsequently replaced by the Scandic Crown Hotel in 1990. The bracket lamp to the left of the Provisions sign is about the position of No. 8, Regent Morton's House, dating from the early sixteenth century. The tenements on the left of the picture (east side) date from after the 1867 Improvement Act when the street, previously known as Blackfriars Wynd, was greatly widened. At the foot of Blackfriars Street, the Cowgate runs left and right, with Infirmary Street straight ahead. On the skyline, the chimney stack (on the left) is part of the now disused Infirmary Street Public Baths, and the lantern cupola (in the centre) is part of St Patrick's Roman Catholic Primary School (now in residential use) in Drummond Street. *Photograph by Duncan McMillan.*

Left. Many of the children in the street have come out to appear in this photograph by J. B. Ross at the beginning of the twentieth century. The photograph was taken in Gloucester Place looking west towards Doune Terrace. *Malcolm Cant Collection.*

Below left. The photograph comes from a picture postcard sent in September 1915 by 'Jim' to his mother, Mrs Winton, of West Nicolson Street, asking her to get him a pair of working boots, 'you no [sic] the kind out of Rankines or Davidson'. Coincidentally, the shop fascia on the left of the picture says 'Davidson & Co., Cash Boot Store'. Perhaps the postcard reminded him of his need! The children, some of whom are barefooted, have congregated at Queen Victoria's statue at the foot of Leith Walk. The statue, completed by John S. Rhind in 1907, had additional panels added in 1913 to commemorate the arrival of the Queen and the Prince Consort at Leith in 1842, and also the departure of the volunteers for the South African War. *Malcolm Cant Collection.*

Below right. The statue of Greyfriars Bobby, on the corner of George IV Bridge and Candlemaker Row, must be one of the most visited in Edinburgh. The story has been told by many Edinburgh writers, including Hamish Coghill in his book *Edinburgh: The Old Town.* Mr Coghill recounts that the dog, Bobby, fulfilled the dual roles of household pet and guard dog to Constable John Gray and his family who lived in the Cowgate. After Gray died in 1858, Bobby was given to returning to the place of burial in Greyfriars Kirkyard to stand guard over his master's grave. He was given food from time to time by locals, especially John Traill, a local restaurant owner, who even took on the task of highlighting the dog's plight when a law was passed ordering that all dogs must either be licensed or destroyed. Lord Provost William Chambers agreed to pay the licence fee himself and had a collar made with the inscription 'Greyfriars Bobby from the Lord Provost, 1867, licensed'. After Bobby died, a donation by Baroness Angela Burdett-Coutts paid for the erection of the bronze statue by William Brodie in 1872, in the form of a drinking fountain which was unveiled on 15 November 1873. The story has been the subject of countless books and a few films, the most recent being *Greyfriars Bobby* starring James Cosmo.

❧ *Right.* Both photographs were taken outside what is now known as the Lord Reid Building, New Assembly Close, at No. 142 High Street. The building, originally opened on 25 June 1814 as the head office of the Commercial Bank of Scotland, incorporated parts of the much older Assembly Rooms of Edinburgh and the King's Arms Tavern.

❧ In January 1894 the Scottish National Society for Prevention of Cruelty to Children (Eastern Branch) opened a Children's Shelter at No. 142 which had previously been called the Trades' Halls. The total cost was £4,000, made up of £2,500 to buy the building and £1,500 to convert it to accommodate the children and various offices. The complex was opened by the Marquis and Marchioness of Tweeddale and remained in the ownership of the Royal Scottish Society for Prevention of Cruelty to Children until 1973. The upper photograph, *c.* 1900, shows the children in the care of two of the staff, surrounded by an interesting array of equipment. The lower picture, dating from the same period, shows the Society officials also at the entrance to No. 142. CHILDREN 1ST has been the working name of the Royal Scottish Society for Prevention of Cruelty to Children since 1995. After the Society vacated the building in 1973, it was again altered and renovated to house the Edinburgh Wax Museum, opened in April 1976. The Museum had three main themes: 'Scotland's History', which contained life-size wax figures of Kings, Queens, Philosophers, Engineers etc; 'Never Never Land', with Humpty-Dumpty, Alice in Wonderland and many more; and the 'Chamber of Horrors' which included Peter Manuel, Madeleine Smith, and Jekyll and Hyde. In 1993 the building was bought by the Faculty of Advocates and completely renovated to create consulting rooms to allow advocates, solicitors and clients to discuss pending litigation. The building takes its name from Lord Reid of Drem (1890-1974) who held several senior legal positions, including Dean of the Faculty of Advocates, 1945-48, before becoming a Lord of Appeal in Ordinary in the House of Lords. *Courtesy of CHILDREN 1ST.*

The Fountain, Starbank Park, Newhaven

❧ *Left.* A welcome piece of open ground at the west end of Newhaven is provided by Starbank Park, laid out at the end of the nineteenth century on the garden ground of Starbank House. The House was the home of the Rev. Walter M. Goalen, founder of Christ Church in Trinity Road. After his death in 1889, Leith Town Council bought the house and gardens which were later linked to the gardens of Laverockbank House to form Starbank Public Park. The central fountain, designed by George Simpson in 1910, was presented to the people of Newhaven by Thomas L. Devlin, J. P., of Newhaven. *Malcolm Cant Collection.*

❧ *Lower left.* The photographer has managed to hold the attention of everyone in this group of children in Duff Street in 1922. At that time, Dalry was a very close-knit community with most of the male population working in one of the many local firms of joiners, builders and engineers. Most of the children in the photograph would have attended either Dalry Primary School or the Normal Practising School, renamed Orwell Primary School in 1975. *Courtesy of Dalry Primary School.*

❧ *Below.* Neill Boyd is in his glory in the company of Jack Milroy at the Carlton Cricket Club in 1963. Several charity matches were played between Carlton and the cast of the 'Five Past Eight Show' which was running at the King's Theatre. Neill, aged five at the time of the photograph, is wearing the uniform of Corstorphine Primary School: he later attended Dundee University and was called to the Scottish Bar in 1983. *Courtesy of Jack Boyd.*

Right. Two young girls walking up Comiston Road past the site now occupied by Greenbank Parish Church, with Greenbank Crescent on the left and Braidburn Terrace on the right. It is difficult to date the photograph as the cable car tracks were not immediately altered when the electric car system was introduced. *Malcolm Cant Collection.*

Below right. Graham Moonie enjoys the safety of the elevated section of Pentland Terrace in May 1930. The car, registration number LB 3067, complete with mudguards, radiator and horn, was a great attraction during visits to see his grandmother, Mrs Margaret Glegg, who lived at No. 11 Pentland Terrace. *Courtesy of Graham Moonie.*

Below. Cissie McPhie, née Koerber, dressed in the height of fashion with her baby daughter, Mary, at Hillend Park on 17 July 1926. *Courtesy of Mrs Mary Burnie, née McPhie.*

Left. Three sisters at the allotments on the south side of Falcon Avenue, *c.* 1926. Before the flats were built on the south side of the Avenue, the ground was occupied as allotments and a tennis court for the use of staff from Jenners in Princes Street. Jones Motor House and the Plaza Ballroom were built on the site of the tennis court in 1926. The girls in the photograph are, from left to right, Violet, Mary and Margaret, who lived with their parents, Maud and Albert, in the flat attached to St Peter's Roman Catholic Church, where Albert was employed as the janitor and sacristan.

Below left. Violet at the allotments in Falcon Avenue, *c.* 1924.

Below centre. Margaret outside No. 70 Falcon Avenue, *c.* 1926.

Below. Falcon Avenue, looking east, towards Falcon Gardens, *c.* 1911, with open ground on the right and flats on the left, constructed from 1893. St Peter's Roman Catholic Church can just be seen at the far end of the Avenue. Outside the church, the only vehicle in the street is a horse-drawn cab belonging to André Raffalovitch, who was a major influence in commissioning Sir Robert Lorimer to design St Peter's. *Malcolm Cant Collection.*

Right. In Cathcart Place, neither the children nor the adults are dressed for summer despite the photograph having been taken on 2 June 1953, the day of the Coronation of Queen Elizabeth II. The street party was organised by the mothers and fathers of the children in the picture, all of whom lived in Cathcart Place. Beetle drives and other fund-raising ventures were organised to raise funds; the cake (on the small table at the bottom of the picture) was baked by the father of one of the children; and tables and chairs were borrowed from the local church. At the end of the party all the children received a crown piece, the girls received a brooch in the form of a crown 'studded with emeralds, rubies, diamonds and sapphires' but it is not known if there was a corresponding gift for the boys. The photograph was taken from the second floor flat of No. 8. *Courtesy of Mrs Betty Styles, née McInnes.*

Below. Nine local girls line up for the curtain opening at one of Gorgie's greatest shows – with a truly international flavour – the Smithfield Street back-green concert of 1951. These informal shows were put on for special events, and during the long summer holidays. From left to right, wearing different national costumes, those featured are: Helen Hood (Spain); Christine Law (USA); Brenda (Turkey); Morag Cameron (Ireland); Harriet Hood, sister of Helen (Holland); Pat Sharp (wearing Indian [Native American] dress); Sheila Bain (Japan); Margaret Liddell (China); Maureen Jolly (Scotland). *Courtesy of Pat Scoular, née Sharp.*

❧ *Above*. Millar Crescent, *c.* 1906, looking east towards Morningside Road, with the curve of Millar Place showing in the bottom right-hand corner of the picture.
Malcolm Cant Collection.

❧ *Left*. In common with many other locations throughout the country, a street party was held in Millar Place on 2 June 1953, the day of the Coronation of Queen Elizabeth II. The group of children and adults all lived in tenement houses in Millar Place, the short cul-de-sac off Millar Crescent. Tables and chairs were borrowed from Braid Parish Church to create an informal auditorium, ideal for watching a Punch and Judy show outside No. 1 Millar Place. *Courtesy of Bill Ovens.*

❧ *Below left*. The Millar family photographed, *c.* 1918, at the studio of James Bacon & Sons, Photographers, No. 130 Princes Street. From left to right: Jack; Alice; James (father); Brooks; Ella; Agnes (née Hunter); Halbert; Muriel; and Arthur, all of No. 37 Morningside Park. James Millar was a builder to trade who was responsible for the redevelopment of the grounds of the East House of the Royal Edinburgh Asylum from 1896. Millar Crescent was built first, followed by Millar Place in 1901 and, thereafter, parts of Morningside Terrace. The builder's yard was at the south end of Morningside Terrace adjacent to the railway line where equipment and materials could be conveniently off-loaded. Many of the first tenement houses in Millar Crescent were intended to be rented to Millar's employees. The firm, established by James Millar in 1894, was involved in the construction of many important buildings in Edinburgh, including: the *Scotsman* offices on North Bridge; F. W. Woolworth's store at the east end of Princes Street; and George Watson's College in Colinton Road.
Courtesy of Eric Millar.

☙ *Right.* Craigview, in Marchhall Road, was built in the late 1870s as a very grand two-storey family home with ornamental ironwork and a pillared balcony over the front entrance. In 1902 the house was allocated the number 1A; in 1908 the address was altered to No. 13 Priestfield Road; and finally, in 1929, to No. 1 Priestfield Road North. The photograph was taken in 1895 when the house was the property of William Penman, a civil engineer, who had trained with Carfrae & Belfrage at No. 1 Erskine Place, and was later in partnership, for a while, with William Allan Carter at No. 5 St Andrew Square. After the partnership ended, Mr Penman had offices at No. 26 Frederick Street until his premature death at Craigview on 20 August 1899. Surviving photographs and papers from the Penman family archive indicate that Mr Penman had an extensive practice throughout Scotland, particularly on the building and reconstruction of bridges. His contracts included: the 1893 reconstruction, with girders, of Lintmill Bridge to replace the original stone arch of 1835; the construction of Boon Bridge, Lauder, 1892-93, a single-span girder structure resting on stone abutments; and a single-span girder bridge, built by Henderson & Duncan, Contractors, at Upper Ford, Abbey St Bathans, also in 1893. In Edinburgh, he was involved in the laying out of the playing fields for the Edinburgh Academy at Inverleith, and for Edinburgh University at Craiglockhart.
Courtesy of Miss Constance MacKenzie, grand-daughter of William Penman.

☙ *Below right.* Mr & Mrs Penman with their surviving family of five daughters and one son, *c.* 1895. Two other children had died in infancy. From left to right: Nell; William Penman; Alice Jane (Dolly); Olive; Gertrude Margaret (Gerty); Mrs Margaret Philippa Penman (née Edgar); Constance Mary (Connie); and John Edgar (Jack). William Penman and Margaret Philippa Edgar married on 18 November 1880 in Dunedin, New Zealand, during a business tour that William undertook from his home town of Edinburgh. Margaret was already resident in New Zealand, her family having moved from Victoria, Australia to Dunedin several years earlier. They returned to Scotland in January 1881 and eventually set up home at Craigview, Marchhall Road. After the death of Mr Penman in 1899, the family moved to No. 14 Rillbank Terrace.
Courtesy of Miss Constance MacKenzie.

🌿 *Above left.* A muzzled, performing bear with its keeper in what is now Priestfield Road North, with Salisbury Crags in the background. The photograph was taken in 1895 by William Penman, hopefully with his young family safely indoors. *Courtesy of Miss Constance MacKenzie.*

🌿 *Above centre.* In the garden of Craigview, Marchhall Road, from left to right: Mrs Margaret Philippa Penman; Alice Jane Penman; Olive Penman; and nurse 'Hattie'. *Courtesy of Miss Constance MacKenzie.*

🌿 *Above.* William Penman relaxing by the fire at his home, Craigview, in Marchhall Road, 1895. *Courtesy of Miss Constance MacKenzie.*

🌿 *Left.* Young Jack Penman, formally dressed in kilt, jacket and school cap, amuses himself by blowing bubbles, watched by his older sister, Alice Jane. *Courtesy of Miss Constance MacKenzie.*

❧ *Right.* The bearded gentleman in the rear seat of the car is John George Bartholomew, with chauffeur Sutton at the wheel, *c.* 1906. The photograph was taken at the side entrance to Falcon Hall, the family home in Morningside. *Courtesy of the Bartholomew family.*

❧ *Below right.* Janet, fourth daughter of Alexander Sinclair Macdonald, farmer in Sutherland, who married John George Bartholomew in 1889. *Courtesy of the Bartholomew family.*

❧ *Below centre.* John George Bartholomew (1860-1920) succeeded his father, John Bartholomew Jnr., in the family map-making business in 1888. At the time, the business shared premises at Park Road with the printers Thomas Nelson & Sons. It was John George who masterminded the transfer of the business in 1911 to purpose-built premises in Duncan Street, Newington, where map production continued for the next eighty-four years, until 1995. *Courtesy of the Bartholomew family.*

❧ *Below.* John George Bartholomew and his wife and family moved from Falcon Hall, in Morningside, to Newington House in Blacket Avenue in 1907 where they remained until 1916. Thereafter, they moved to Cardon in Mortonhall Road. The photograph, taken in the garden of Newington House in 1908, shows the whole family, from left to right: *back row*; Louis St Clair; John; Janet; and Hugh; *front row*; Margaret; Elizabeth; and John George. *Courtesy of the Bartholomew family.*

❧ *Above left.* The Bartholomew firm held annual outings, one of which was a picnic for the staff and their families to Falcon Hall. *Courtesy of the Bartholomew family.*

❧ *Below left.* Dr John Bartholomew (1890-1962) Geographer and Cartographer Royal, working on the mid-twentieth century edition of *The Times Atlas of the World,* published in five volumes between 1955 and 1960. The first edition had been edited by John's father, Dr John George, and published in 1922. Dr John was assisted by his three sons who took over the running of the firm on his death: John C. as cartographer; Peter H. as chairman; and Robert G. as production director. *Courtesy of the Bartholomew family.*

❧ *Below.* Falcon Hall, on the Canaan estate, was owned and named by Alexander Falconar who commissioned Thomas Hamilton to extend and remodel an earlier house built on the site in 1780 for Lord Provost William Coulter. Falcon Hall was a grand building of two principal storeys with a façade of twelve Corinthian monolithic pillars. On either side of the entrance were statues of Nelson and Wellington and falcons sat above the cornice. The Falconars were generous benefactors in the community, in particular to the first Morningside Parish Church and Christ Church Episcopal. The Bartholomew family lived at Falcon Hall from 1900 until just before 1907 when the building was demolished. Part of the frontage, however, was saved, and moved, stone by stone, and re-erected as the frontage of Bartholomew's new business premises in Duncan Street. *Courtesy of the Bartholomew family.*

❧ *Right.* Wedding party at Gorgie House, Gorgie Road, in 1934. From left to right: Willie Blane; Harry Affleck; Ada Macarthur; Gladys Macarthur; Lilly Affleck; and the Rev. John Spence Ewen, minister of Liberton Parish Church. The Macarthur family owned and ran the Station Bar in Gorgie Road. The stables attached to Gorgie House were also used in connection with the family's interest in horse riding. *Courtesy of Mrs Sheila Scott and Mrs Linda Duffy.*

❧ *Below right.* Wedding party at Haymarket Church, Dalry Road, in 1955, at the marriage of Ann Steel and Ian Clark. The bridesmaid was Joan Steel and the best man was Douglas Watson who married each other on 27 August 1956. *Malcolm Cant Collection.*

❧ *Below.* A rather formal pose, similar in style to many studio photographs of the period, is adopted by Ena Leask and David Anderson on their wedding day in 1927. The photograph was taken at the studio of J. R. Coltart of No. 8 Dalmeny Street after the wedding ceremony at Leith St Paul's Church in Lorne Street. *Courtesy of Mrs Linda Pittilo, née Anderson.*

Left. Alexander Dobson Snr and his wife Isabella (née Stewart) seated at either side of the table at No. 21 Mayfield Road, in 1904, on their fortieth wedding anniversary. Isabella is holding her grandson, Alexander Dobson Hunter, and Alexander is holding another grandson, William Alexander Dobson Hunter. *Courtesy of Mrs Pauline Matthews.*

Below left. A study in concentration at Harrison Park in the summer of 1939. From left to right: Mrs Frances Wilson; Mrs Agnes Glasgow; and Mrs Annie Wilson, mother-in-law of Frances. *Photograph by Frank Wilson.*

Below. This unusual photograph was taken, *c.* 1920, at the Cameron Toll signal box on the track between Newington and Craigmillar. The lady in the centre is Jessie Ann (Dette) Deuchars, whose father, David Deuchars, was a high-ranking official in the London and North Eastern Railway Company. *Courtesy of David Deuchars.*

❧ *Right.* Sir Peter Findlay, his wife Helen, and their daughter, Caroline, lived at West Grange. Sir Peter, and several members of his family before him, was a proprietor of the *Scotsman* newspaper at the time when Roy Thomson took control. *Courtesy of Mrs Louise Jenkins, née Nicol.*

❧ *Below right.* In the bottom left-hand corner of the picture, West Grange is the large detached property with the bow-fronted windows on either side of the west-facing entrance. Blackford Avenue runs along the bottom edge of the photograph to meet Grange Loan on the left. The other large building, to the east of West Grange, is the Artesian Well, sunk in 1889 by William Younger & Co. Ltd., of Holyrood Breweries. *Courtesy of Simmons Aerofilms Ltd.*

❧ *Below.* John and Jean Nicol, née Inglis, with their daughter, Louise, at West Grange in July 1939 when they lived in the adjacent lodge house. John Nicol was in the employ of Sir Peter Findlay before the Second World War, and thereafter as a member of staff at the *Scotsman.* When the Nicols were resident at the lodge house, Sir Peter kept Chinese ducks and a penguin, named Sammy, that lived in a pond near to the greenhouses which can be seen in the background. *Courtesy of Mrs Louise Jenkins, née Nicol.*

❧ *Above.* Mary Carmichael (left) and her sister, Margaret, *c.* 1906, near Mid Lodge, Glenlockhart Road. *Malcolm Cant Collection.*

❧ *Top left.* The open window of the ground floor flat at No. 7 Caledonian Place provides the ideal setting for a family photograph, *c.* 1925. From left to right: Mrs Kathleen Deuchars; her daughter Evelyn; and her son Andrew. Both children attended Dalry Primary School. *Photograph by Frank Wilson.*

❧ *Far left.* The very latest technology, the delayed exposure, captures Frances and Frank Wilson in Colinton Dell around the time of their marriage in July 1930. Frank Wilson spent most of his working life with Scott Morton, the cabinetmakers, in Murieston Road. He was also a very enthusiastic amateur photographer whose work has been shown in several books on the social history of Edinburgh. Frances was a hairdresser who worked in Santou Hairdressing Salon in Shandwick Place before she was married. *Photograph by Frank Wilson.*

❧ *Left.* Dolls have not yet been abandoned in this 1947 group in the back green of Nos. 16, 18 and 20 Ogilvie Terrace. From left to right: Moira Alexander; Morag Newlands; Catherine Newlands (sister of Morag); Louise Wilson; Sheila Alexander (twin of Moira).

Right. An idyllic spot for a quiet bit of fishing: Nell Hannah at Bog's Mill, Colinton Dell, in 1904. Less than a decade earlier, in 1898, the author John Geddie in *The Home Country of R. L. Stevenson* described the area around Boag's Mill as 'one of the prettiest and most secluded of the riverside nooks'. Bog's, or Boag's, Mill, dating from the late sixteenth century, ground grain and made paper and snuff. It also produced the first bank notes manufactured in Scotland 'a picquet of soldiers mounting guard in the cottage above'. *Courtesy of June Clark.*

Below right. Twenty years later, Nell Hannah is reduced to a supporting role only, holding her first-born child, Marion, behind the net curtain on the right-hand side of the picture. The main show, however, is the children of Bruce Street, off Balcarres Street, in Morningside, in 1924, with some well-heeled boys in the front row. *Courtesy of June Clark.*

Below. Mrs Mary Koerber at the home of her daughter, Cissie, at No. 5 Ryehill Terrace in the mid-1930s. Mrs Koerber was the proprietor of a 'wet' fish shop in Leith. *Courtesy of Mrs Mary Burnie, née McPhie.*

[A] Two cheeky 'monkeys' and two wee angels at Fort Saughton, Saughton Public Park, in 1991: on the left, Claire, aged 6, and on the right, Gillian, aged 4. *Courtesy of Pat and Douglas Scoular.*

[B] Karen O'Brien with her first daughter, Joanna, aged 2, feeding Canada geese at Duddingston Loch in 1996. *Photograph by Jenni Wood.*

[C] Out on the open road, in the west of Edinburgh, Abbie Irvine, riding Weeta, on the left, and Kathryn O'Brien, riding Marigold, on the right. *Photograph by Peter Stubbs.*

[A]

[B]

[C]

[D]

OVERHEARD DOWN GORGIE WAY.

THE LAIRD —
AM I AW RICHT NOO FOR THE
EXHIBEESHUN, BOY.
THE LADDIE —
OH AY, THEY'RE NO VERY
PARTICULAR DOON AT THE
EXHIBITION.

[E]

SHOOTING THE CHUTE AT THE
EXHIBITION.
MY WORD' I'M OFF"

TO THE
WATER CHUTE.

Donald McGill

[A], [B] and [C] These three photographs are from a commemorative booklet produced for the International Exhibition of Industry, Science and Art on the Meadows in 1886. From top to bottom: the Bandstand; the Concert Hall; and the Central Court. *Courtesy of Tom Brand.*

[D] and [E] Humorous postcards were very popular covering various aspects of the Scottish National Exhibition at Saughton in 1908. *Malcolm Cant Collection.*

[A]

[B]

[C]

[D]

[E]

[F]

[A] The Make Poverty History March, on Saturday 2 July 2005, started at the south end of Middle Meadow Walk. It attracted many thousands of people either as marchers or spectators.

[B] The March was led by several civic, religious and business leaders, three of whom were photographed on Jaw Bone Walk shortly before the March began. From left to right: Cardinal Keith O'Brien; Sir Tom Farmer; and Cardinal Cormac Murphy-O'Connor.

[C] Although the March was late in starting, the participants were not long in reaching Forrest Road where several people needed extra bottles of water from the local shops.

[D] This African percussion band led the parade with only a few stoppages over the entire route from the Meadows, via George IV Bridge to Princes Street and back to the Meadows via Castle Terrace and Lady Lawson Street.

[E] An army of Socialistworld supporters make a strong statement with their red banners at the top of Middle Meadow Walk.

[F] In Princes Street the March is by no means over and the participants are still going strong, encouraged by a good turnout of spectators.

All Malcolm Cant Collection.

[A] The North Wind Victorian Street Organ with its operator, John Pettigrew, at the Gorgie Dalry Gala Day in Murieston Park on 10 June 2006.

[B] The Edinburgh Samba School performing at the 25th Gorgie Dalry Gala Day at Murieston Park in 2005.

[C] The Stepping Out School of Dance put on an elegant display at the Gorgie Dalry Gala Day at Murieston Park in 2003.

Photographs by Bryan Montgomery.

[B]

[A]

[C]

28

PART 2: AT LEISURE, SCHOOL AND CHURCH

Part 2 has 85 photographs relating to leisure, schools and churches. The section on leisure begins with various photographs of the city centre which has always been the main area of tourist attraction. These photographs include several 1950s shots taken by the photographer, Norward Inglis, who lived and worked at No. 18 Regent Terrace. His subjects include Princes Street, the Gardens, the Ross Bandstand and the Floral Clock.

Many of the main sporting activities of the City are covered, including: the redoubtable Miss Carswell about to make her tour of inspection at Swanston Golf Course; the North British Rubber Company Tennis Club at Craiglockhart; Francie and Josie in a completely different line-up at the Carlton Cricket Club; boating at Cramond and St Margaret's Loch; the Grove Swimming Club and the staff of Dalry Baths; throwing the hammer at the Highland Games at Murrayfield; and a couple of interesting football teams – Leith Emmet and Leith Ivanhoe. Pages 42 and 43 are devoted to cycling from which it is clear that the popularity, practicality and versatility of the bicycle has been with us for many years. There are also a couple of photographs taken at the time of the Scottish National Exhibition which was held in 1908 in the grounds of Saughton Hall Mansion, now Saughton Public Park.

There is also a wide selection of pictures relating to music, drama and dance, such as the

The Lawnmarket, with its interesting mix of narrow closes, outside stairs and traditional shop fronts, has always been a great attraction for tourists and residents alike. This mid-1950s photograph is taken on the north side of the street looking towards the Tron Kirk and St Giles Cathedral. J. H. Telford, the fruiterer, at No. 459 has a sign that mimics the spire of St Giles', and H. B. Wyllie, the chemist, at No. 463 has the mortar and pestle.
Photograph by Duncan McMillan.

amateur group with the very professional name of the Nessie Hynd Crown Troupe of Speciality Dancers from Leith. Orchestras are also included: the Blue Hungry Band from Juniper Green probably never attained the rank of 'orchestra' but John Henry Cooke's Royal Circus Orchestra certainly did in Edinburgh's East Fountainbridge. From the world stage there are pictures of Kathleen Ferrier, Bruno Walter and Ernest Ansermet at the Usher Hall during the Edinburgh International Festival. The picture of the Society Ball at the Assembly Rooms is well documented but, unfortunately, the exact occasion of the social dance at the Plaza Ballroom in Morningside has not been identified even although Norward Inglis, the photographer, appears in it as a young man.

The section on schools occupies ten pages, with particular emphasis on sport and extra-curricular activities. Obviously, all schools have not been included but hopefully the selection is reasonably representative of most types of educational establishments. Tennis and golf are included at Boroughmuir School and club drill at Dr Guthrie's School at Liberton. Vocational subjects such as book binding, woodwork, metal casting, laundry and cooking are represented by Milton House School and Tynecastle. Pageantry and display have been provided by Gillespie's, Donaldson's Hospital, Corstorphine and Leith

Academy, and playground scenes by Grange Home School, Esdaile, Roseburn and Morningside. One or two special occasions are also included i.e. when Queen Elizabeth II visited The Edinburgh Academy on the occasion of the school's 150th anniversary and when the Moderator of the General Assembly of the Church of Scotland visited Esdaile School on Moderator's Day. The ever-popular class photograph is represented by Gilmore Place Public School, the Misses Watt's Private School at Liberton, Victoria School, Warrender Park School and St Trinnean's. School staff photographs include Boroughmuir, Craigmount (in Dick Place), and Davidson's Mains.

A smaller, but equally interesting, selection has been made of photographs relating to various church activities, including choirs and a christening. Special commemorative occasions include the lifting of the tenor bell at St Cuthbert's at the West End, and the laying of the foundation stone at Greenbank United Free Church, later Greenbank Parish Church. Sunday School picnics include Colinton Parish Church on a barge on the Union Canal. The section concludes with photographs of children playing in the manse garden of the original Morningside Parish Church in Morningside Road, and the Women's Guild, full strength, outside the Cairns Memorial Church in Gorgie Road ready to go on their annual outing.

The Nessie Hynd Crown Troupe of Speciality Dancers was 'Crowned with Success' on 10 February 1906. The photograph, taken at Paterson's Burgh Studio at No. 31 Great Junction Street, shows, from left to right: Nessie Hynd; Barbara Leask; Ena Leask; Beatrice Young; and Willie Hynd. *Courtesy of Linda Pittilo, née Anderson.*

In this 1950s picture, travellers and passers-by appear relatively relaxed at the notoriously cold and windy Waverley Steps between the North British Hotel (now the Balmoral) and the ornamental roof garden of the Waverley Market. *Photograph by Norward Inglis.*

One of Edinburgh's most traditional views with Robert Adam's Register House on the left and the equestrian statue of Wellington by Sir John Steell on the right. In Waterloo Place there is a very long queue for the tramcar at one of the island stops. *Photograph by Norward Inglis.*

❧ *Above.* The long promenade between St John's Episcopal Church at the West End and the Floral Clock at the Mound has long been a popular venue for strollers, or for those resting on the many memorial benches. On Princes Street, the ornate stonework of the former Palace Hotel can be seen to the left of the trees. *Photograph by Norward Inglis.*

❧ *Above left.* The Scott Monument dominates this 1950s photograph of Princes Street, looking west at the junction with Waverley Bridge. The street's natural elegance has not yet been compromised by its latter-day clutter of signs, road markings and badly aligned pavement extensions. *Photograph by Norward Inglis.*

❧ *Left.* Traffic management at the West End of Edinburgh has occupied the minds of the city planners for many decades, especially the problem of giving vehicular access from Shandwick Place to Queensferry Street. In this photograph a compromise has been reached by allowing tramcar access only, with relative safety maintained for strolling pedestrians. The photograph is undated but the handrails were erected in 1948 and had been replaced by a series of raised flower beds by January 1952. *Photograph by Norward Inglis.*

Right. West Princes Street Gardens was originally private ground, leased from the City in 1816 by the proprietors of houses in Princes Street between Hanover Street and Hope Street. Prior to the construction of the railway below the Castle rock, the gardens were much more extensive and included ground to the south of the Castle on which Johnstone Terrace was later built. In 1876, when the gardens were re-acquired by the City, Robert Morham, the City Architect, redesigned the layout and added the picturesque red sandstone cottage at the east side. The photograph, dated 1905, shows a huge crowd around the rather rudimentary bandstand.

Below right. In 1935 the City replaced the old bandstand with the stone-built Ross Bandstand complete with dance floor and raised seating. The small board propped against the centre of the raised platform says: 'NO CROSSING PLATFORM DURING PERFORMANCES'. The facilities have been improved over the years but at the present day they are hopelessly inadequate for the type of shows now presented. *Malcolm Cant Collection.*

Below. The photographer, Norward Inglis, captures Sir Walter Scott in the distance, and Professor John Wilson, pen name Christopher North, on the left, both looking resolutely nor'wards, while the best animation award for the contestants on the park bench looks as though it might go to a photo finish. *Photograph by Norward Inglis.*

Left. The south-facing Scottish American War Memorial in West Princes Street Gardens creates a comfortable spot from which to watch the world go by and to listen to the band at the Ross Bandstand nearby. The First World War memorial, unveiled in 1927, was erected by Scots of American descent. The seated, kilted figure, entitled 'The Call' by R. Tait MacKenzie of Pennsylvania University, was cast at the Roman Bronze Works in Brooklyn, USA, and is believed to be a likeness of one of MacKenzie's students, Granville Carrel. The stonework was by Colin C. Macandrew & Partners Ltd., of Edinburgh. *Photograph by Norward Inglis.*

Below. Edinburgh's Floral Clock, the first of its kind in Britain, began ticking on 10 June 1903. Initially, there was an hour hand only, the minute hand being added in 1904. The basic mechanism was salvaged from Elie Parish Church in Fife and rebuilt by James Ritchie & Son (Clockmakers) Ltd., of Edinburgh, who have maintained the clock ever since. It required to be wound every day until it was converted to electric power in 1973. Apparently it was the task of one of Ritchie's apprentices to wind the clock early every morning, including Sundays, but it was not unheard of for a resourceful apprentice to give the clock a few turns late on a Saturday (when he was in town anyway!) so that the Sunday winding could be done at a more respectable hour. The original machinery, with weights similar to a long-case clock, was housed in a small room under the statue of Allan Ramsay. An additional mechanism was added in 1905 to reproduce the call of the cuckoo but it was not until shortly after 1950 that an operating model of a cuckoo was installed.

The photograph, taken in 1950, commemorates the 100th anniversary of the birth of Robert Louis Stevenson. Over the years, many events have been commemorated including: 1911, a Floral Crown for George V; 1940, 603 City of Edinburgh Squadron of the Auxiliary Air Force; 1956, The Faculty of Actuaries in Scotland Centenary; 1965, The Salvation Army Centenary; 1971, Sir Walter Scott, 1771–1832; 1985, 75th Anniversary of the Girl Guides; and 1996, Robert Burns Bicentenary. More than 25,000 individual plants are used every year. The story of the Floral Clock was written in 1998 by Malcolm Fife in his booklet, *Princes Street Gardens: The Floral Clock. Photograph by Norward Inglis.*

❧ *Right*. Miss Margaret Carswell of Swanston Golf Club, on the right, is about to begin her tour of the course, apparently oblivious to the dangers of driving off before the pin (of the tailboard) has been replaced in the hole. Miss Carswell established the course in 1927 at a time when she, and her female contemporaries, found that many of Edinburgh's golf clubs were confined to male members only. When the club was first established, Miss Carswell insisted that only female members were to be admitted, but the rule was relaxed many years later when the existing female members were keen to admit their husbands and male friends. *Courtesy Ellen and Jim McLagan*.

❧ *Below right*. The North British Rubber Co. Ltd., of Castle Mills, off Dundee Street had tennis courts for the use of the staff in Colinton Road on ground which backed on to the Union Canal near Meggetland. The photograph shows the 1930 team at Colinton Road. The only members of the team positively identified are Willie Fraser, in the centre of the back row, and Mary Ritchie, second from the right in the front row, who married one another in 1941. *Courtesy of Patricia Davidson*.

❧ *Below*. Jack Milroy (Francie) and Rikki Fulton (Josie) at the Carlton Cricket Ground in 1963 when Carlton took on the cast of the 'Five Past Eight Show' which was running at the King's Theatre at the time. The columns of the Artesian Well in Grange Loan can be seen in the background. *Courtesy of Jack Boyd*.

Left. The Water Chute was a leading attraction at the 1908 Exhibition beside the figure-8 railway built by T. M. Hartin & Co. of Pittsburgh, USA. Those two attractions and the various tournaments, pageants, displays and balloon ascents all contributed to excellent daily attendances. *Malcolm Cant Collection*.

Below left. The fairground, photographed here in 1984, has been an integral part of the Meadows Festival since inception. *Photograph by A. C. Robson*.

Below. The Helter Skelter was a great attraction at the Scottish National Exhibition which was held, in 1908, in the grounds of Saughton Hall Mansion, now Saughton Public Park. The exhibition attracted a wide variety of interests from throughout the United Kingdom, France, Italy, Denmark, Holland, Russia, Serbia, Persia, Japan, China, the USA and Canada. The main topics included Scottish Industries, Nursing, Education, Agriculture, Farming, and Artisans' Work. Near the Balgreen Road entrance there was also a large, dome-roofed concert hall, with a horse-shoe shaped gallery, a three-manual organ by Abbot & Smith of Leeds, and a 'fairy fountain' which produced an interesting rainbow effect when lit. Between 1 May and 31 October total admissions to the exhibition were 3.5 million. *Malcolm Cant Collection*.

Moulin Rouge or Helter Skelter, Scottish National Exhibition, Edinburgh, 1908.

Right. This 1950s photograph of the mouth of the River Almond shows Lord Rosebery's estate on the left bank and the boat houses of the Cramond Boat Club on the right. The boats are all pleasure craft as the Almond's working boats disappeared from the river many years previously. At one time there were several working mills, including Cockle, Fair-a-Far, Craigie's, Peggy's and Dowie's. *Photograph by Norward Inglis.*

Below right. Just below Cramond Brig, an idyllic boating scene with a ratio of one oarsman to four passengers. Prior to the construction of Queensferry Road, west of Blackhall, the road to Queensferry crossed Cramond Brig which still carries a rudimentary maintenance schedule cut into the parapet stonework: 'repaired by both shires, 1687, 1761, 1776 and 1854. *Courtesy of Cramond Heritage Trust.*

Below. St Margaret's Loch, in Holyrood Park, was not formed at the end of the last Ice Age but was constructed artificially in 1857 at the suggestion of Prince Albert to improve the general drainage. When this photograph was taken in the early 1950s, the loch was a popular boating pond. The ruined St Anthony's Chapel above the loch is believed to date from the early fifteenth century. *Photograph by Norward Inglis.*

Left. The staff of Dalry Baths on the entrance steps on the south side of Caledonian Crescent in 1905, with superintendent Baillie (father of Charlie Baillie, the Olympic swimmer) in the centre. The poster in the background announces an Annual Gala at Dalry Baths on Friday 14 October by the Edinburgh Swimming Club and Humane Society. Mr Baillie and his family lived in a small flat incorporated into the west side of the baths complex. The apparently large staff shown in the picture was probably required because of the high number of private baths in operation which were labour-intensive to maintain and operate. The hot, private baths were very popular with local people whose houses were originally built without baths. Patrons could choose between first class at 1/3d (6p) and second class at 9d (4p), both of which lasted for half an hour. First-class patrons had the luxury of unlimited hot water whereas those opting for second class had to make do with the bath being filled once only. A small piece of carbolic soap was provided free, but more refined soap, and towels, could be hired for a small sum. When it was busy the attendants chalked the expiry times on the outside of the doors to remind them when to call 'time'. *Courtesy of Tommy Jamieson.*

Below left. Members of the Grove Swimming Club photographed in 1921 on an outing, possibly to Portobello, with Charlie Baillie, the Olympic swimmer on the extreme left of the picture. Dalry Baths have been the home of the Grove Swimming Club since its inauguration in the first decade of the twentieth century under its first patron, the Marquis of Linlithgow. Over the years, the Grove has had many good swimmers but none better than Charlie Baillie, born in 1902, who was Scottish champion in the 50 and 100 yards championship every year from 1920 to 1926. He also won several English championships when he later moved to Oldham. The highlight of his career was, however, the 1924 Paris Olympics, the Games in which Eric Liddell, of *Chariots of Fire* fame also competed. Unfortunately, Charlie was beaten in the heats but the experience remained with him for the remainder of his long life. *Courtesy of Tom Scott's family.*

Right. These eight musicians formed the John Henry Cooke's Royal Circus Orchestra, photographed in Edinburgh sometime between 1902 and 1906. The gentleman in the centre of the picture, with the cornet and conductor's baton, is Harry Dale who was Cooke's musical director for many years. He took the stage name, Harry Wamba, to differentiate himself from his father, also Harry Dale, who was a music hall artiste, vocalist, circus jester and, latterly, a circus manager. The location of the photograph is not known, but having regard to the formal dress and the presence of heavy musical instruments, it is possible that it was taken at the rear of Cooke's Circus in East Fountainbridge. Cooke opened his Royal Circus in 1886. After his retirement in 1911, the building became a picture house until 1932, and thereafter the Palladium Theatre. *Courtesy of Colin Dale, grandson of Harry Wamba.*

Below right. J. F. Wyllie's Happy Family Ponies are getting to know their audience for Cinderella at the King's Theatre opening night on 8 December 1906. *Malcolm Cant Collection.*

Below. The 'World Famous Blue Hungry Band' pauses for a photograph beside Juniper Green Primary School. They may well have been world famous but details of their exploits have not survived. *Courtesy of Gordon Renwick.*

❧ *Left*. Contestant No. 22, G. E. Mitchell of the Glasgow Police throwing the hammer on 3 September 1949 at the Highland Games at Murrayfield. *Photograph by Norward Inglis.*

❧ *Below left*. Leith Emmet Football Club, 1911–12, winners of the Brown Cup, photographed near Chancelot Mill, off Ferry Road. Back row, left to right: J. Galbraith; A. Dorance, President; P. Keenan. Middle row, left to right: W. Brady; J. McAbe; A. Meaney; J. Stevenson; J. McCran; J. Berry; J. Meaney. Front row, P. Munro; A. Berry; T. Baillie; C. Brunton, Captain; T. Boucher; Jas. Meaney, Secretary. *Courtesy of Mrs Jean McCran.*

❧ *Below*. Leith Ivanhoe Football Club, 1913–14, winners of the King Cup 1911–12, 1912–13, 1913–14, the Moir Cup in 1913–14 and the Leith & District Cup 1913–14. Back row, left to right: J. Galbraith; J. Berry; R. Henderson; J. Young; D. Henderson. Middle row, left to right: T. Simpson, Masseur; A. Hogg, Secretary; J. McCran; W. Millar; P. Whyte; R. Stewart; P. Ramsay; E. Bridges; A. Moyes, Vice President; W. Mackenzie, Trainer. Front row, left to right: A. Berry; C. Brunton; J. Blyth, Captain; J. R. Burden, Hon. Pres.; H. Cullen; F. Forbes; J. Christie. *Courtesy of Mrs Jean McCran.*

❧ *Right*. James Hunter, at the front, and his co-rider, Willie Smith, at Loanhead on the Hunter Special built by James Hunter. He won the Waverley Roads Club gold medal in 1897 for covering 100 miles in 5 hours and 25 minutes. James Hunter, a blacksmith to trade, was the father of William Hay Hunter who established W. H. Hunter (Motors) Ltd., of Morningside. *Courtesy of Bill Hunter.*

❧ *Below right*. Cissie (Sarah) Koerber with her bicycle and books on the east side of Castle Street, *c.* 1920. The photograph was taken outside the premises of Douglas & Foulis, the booksellers, where Cissie was employed as an assistant. Part of her duties was to deliver book orders, by bicycle, to various New Town addresses. The substantial building, in the top left-hand corner of the picture, is occupied by the Royal Exchange Assurance Corporation at No. 8. *Courtesy of Linda Pittilo, née Anderson.*

❧ *Below*. James Millar, of Restalrig Terrace, complete with bow tie, pocket handkerchief and watch chain, photographed (with his bicycle) by Halkett of Portobello in the 1880s. Mr Millar was in partnership as an undertaker in Great Junction Street, and was also a governor at Trinity Academy.
Courtesy of Mrs Mary Burnie, née McPhie.

Left. Children can be endlessly resourceful, given two wheels, a stout plank, an oil drum and a few bricks to prevent the drum from rolling away at the crucial moment. The much greater risk of injury appears to be from the precarious position of some of the partly demolished masonry in the houses of Saunders Street and India Place which were taken down in the 1960s. The houses had been allowed to deteriorate badly but, in retrospect, they were probably needlessly demolished. Both India Place and Saunders Street dated from the 1820s. *Photograph by the late John K. Wilkie.*

Below left. On the left, Alfred Grant, at the time Group Pensions Manager of the Scottish Widows' Fund, accompanied by his son. They are talking to Louise Wilson, a clerkess with the same firm, who is facing the camera, with Bobby Davies on the extreme right of the picture. The photograph was taken, *c.* 1957, at the Cyclists' Touring Club stand at the Hobbies' Exhibition in the Waverley Market.

Below. Louise Wilson, in the uniform of Craiglockhart School, shows off her very first bike, a powder blue BSA, fitted with the temporary addition of wooden blocks on the pedals. The photograph was taken, *c.* 1946, in Harrison Park. *Photograph by Frank Wilson.*

❧ This unidentified occasion for formal dress was held at the Plaza Ballroom in Morningside Road, *c.* 1939. Norward Inglis, whose photographic work appears in this book, is the young man facing the camera on the left of the photograph. His mother, Jean Inglis, née Taylor, is the lady with the glasses on the extreme left. The only other people definitely identified are James Burgess (third from the right) and Margaret Grindlay (seated third from the right). The Plaza Ballroom opened in September 1926 and closed after the last waltz on Saturday 1 March 1975. *Courtesy of Barbara Simpson.*

Left. The third Edinburgh International Festival, in 1949, included a recital at the Usher Hall by Kathleen Ferrier with Bruno Walter as her accompanist, described as 'an unforgetable occasion' in *Edinburgh Festival: A Preview of the First Ten Years, 1947–1956. Photograph by Norward Inglis.*

Below left. During the same Festival, in 1949, there was a symphony concert at the Usher Hall by Orchestre De La Suisse Romande, conducted by Ernst Ansermet, with soloists Jacqueline Blancard and Henri Honegger. The growing internationality of the Festival was also recognised that year by the inclusion of ballet from France and two German ensembles – the Berlin Philharmonic Orchestra and the Düsseldorf Theatre Company, led by Gustaf Gründgens. At the end of the 1949 Festival, the Society reluctantly released its first Artistic Director, Rudolf Bing, to the Metropolitan Opera. *Photograph by Norward Inglis.*

Below. On Tuesday 23 June 1953 a Presentation Ball was held at the Assembly Rooms in George Street, sponsored by the British Legion in Scotland. The photograph shows, from left to right: Lady George Montagu Douglas Scott; the Countess of Home (wife of the 14th Earl of Home who, in 1963, renounced his peerages to fight the Perth & Kinross by-election and become British Prime Minister); and the Countess of Dalkeith (whose husband became 9th Duke of Buccleuch and 11th Duke of Queensberry in 1973).
Photograph by Norward Inglis.

❧ *Above*. Boys learning the craft of bookbinding and tooling at Milton House School in the Canongate in 1935. According to the Educational Directories of the day, Milton House Primary School was under the control of the head teacher, Alexander Watt, and Milton House Technical Institute which catered for Continuation Classes in the evening, was headed by Alexander Reid. *From* Edinburgh Education Week, *1936*.

❧ *Right*. The two, rather posed, photographs, opposite, show pupils at James Gillespie's School in Gillespie Crescent when it was under the control of the Merchant Company of Edinburgh. *Above*. A very large class of girls in the sewing and needlework class. *Below*. A smaller, younger group going through their paces at the dance and callisthenics class. When James Gillespie, the snuff manufacturer from Spylaw House in Colinton, died in 1797 he left the greater part of his estate for 'the erection and endowment of a Hospital for aged men and women and a Free School for poor boys', to be managed by the Edinburgh Merchant Company as trustees. They built Gillespie's Hospital in 1802 in Gillespie Crescent and a school for boys in 1803 on a site nearby. In 1870 the boys' school was moved to the Gillespie Crescent building. In 1908 the administration of the school was passed to the Edinburgh School Board, and a few years later, in 1914, the pupils (by then boys and girls) were moved to the building in Warrender Park Crescent, vacated by Boroughmuir School when they moved to Viewforth. The Gillespie Crescent building was later occupied by the Royal Blind Asylum and demolished in 1974. At the present day, James Gillespie's Primary School and High School are both situated on the Bruntsfield House complex, off Whitehouse Loan. *Courtesy of James Gillespie's High School.*

❧ *Top*. Mrs Elsie Burnie, nursery teacher, supervising a group of children in the garden at Grange Home School, *c.* 1969. *Courtesy of Mrs Elsie Burnie.*

❧ *Middle*. A class of boys and girls, and a canine friend, at Grange Home School in 1934. *Courtesy of the late Mrs A Wilkinson, née Morley Smith.*

❧ *Lower*. Staff and pupils of Grange Home School photographed on the tennis court at the south end of the school grounds in the early 1950s. *Courtesy of Mrs Kathleen Biggers.*

❧ In 1920, Mrs Edith Morley Smith, a First World War widow, bought No. 9 Strathearn Place for herself and her four children where she opened the first Grange Home School. She moved the school to Dunard at No. 123 Grange Loan in 1933 which remained there until 1939 when the school was evacuated to Berwickshire and later Perthshire. Unfortunately Dunard was badly damaged when it was requisitioned by the War Department, as a result of which Mrs Morley Smith decided to retire in 1946, leaving the running of the school to her daughter, Miss Joan Morley Smith. During the following three decades Grange Home School increased its roll to almost 150 day pupils between the ages of three and eleven years. Girls remained at the school until eleven but the boys moved to other schools at age seven. When the school closed in 1973 the building was let to St Margaret's School who used it as their senior boarding house. St Margaret's bought the building in 1976 and later sold it to developers who converted the original house to flats and built four other blocks in the garden ground. The original building, always known as Dunard, was designed by the architect, Robert R. Raeburn, around 1865 and was owned between 1895 and 1913 by Sir Robert Cranston, Lord Provost of Edinburgh. Sir Robert entered the Town Council in 1892, was City Treasurer from 1899–1902 and Lord Provost in 1903. He was knighted by Edward VII in May 1903.

Tynecastle High School, in McLeod Street, was opened as Tynecastle Supplementary School on 3 September 1912 with fifteen teachers recruited from various Edinburgh schools including Dalry, Gorgie, and North Merchison. More than 500 pupils enrolled, mainly from Craiglockhart School, Dalry School and Gorgie School, but there was insufficient furniture for such a large intake which meant that only twelve classrooms were ready for occupation. Despite these initial setbacks the formal opening by the Rt. Hon. Alexander Ure, Lord Advocate, went ahead as planned on 16 November 1912. By 1914 there were 25 classes with an average school roll of 790 pupils. From the very beginning Tynecastle was a new venture for the Edinburgh School Board, concentrating on technical subjects and equipped with all the latest machinery in a range of workshops beside the main building. Subjects taught included joinery, plumbing, cobbling, haircutting, engineering, plastering, laundering, sewing, cooking, and housewifery. The academic subjects were taught in the main building where the boys and girls were strictly segregated up to the leaving age of fourteen. The photographs shown here date from the first decade of the school's existence. At the present day there are imminent plans to construct a completely new school on the opposite side of McLeod Street.

Top. Tenon saws, jack planes and sawing boards are all in evidence in this well-equipped woodwork room in Tynecastle School.

Middle. Equally committed are the girls in the laundry class working through a large basket of items using unwieldy sadirons.

Below right. The casting workshop is a hive of activity with various castings being worked on at floor level and a huge crucible being manoeuvred into position.

Below. The cooking class with the girls working to a recipe for 'Roly-Poly'.
All courtesy of Tynecastle High School.

Left. This group of rather serious-looking female tennis players formed the match team for Boroughmuir Tennis Club in 1909. The photograph was taken at the front of Viewpark Cottage in Warrender Park Crescent where the photographers, A. Swan Watson, had their office and studio. At that time Boroughmuir School occupied the adjacent building which was later used by James Gillespie's High School for Girls. From left to right: *back row*, Eva Cowe; Susie Newlands; Jane Johnston; Isabella McIntosh; Daisy Grieve; *front row*, Rhoda Graham; Lena Mackay (Secretary); Agnes Sutherland (Captain); Emma Young (Vice-captain); Daisy Harrison. *Courtesy of Boroughmuir High School.*

Below left. Equally serious looking is the boys' match team for Boroughmuir Golf Club at the same location in 1909. From left to right: *back row*, G. Anderson; A. Forbes; J. Erskine; Ed Hislop; W. F. Doughty; T. Wylie; *front row*, T. Scott; D. Mein; J.S. Parker (Secretary); W. Seaton (Captain); J. Angus; H. Emslie. *Courtesy of Boroughmuir High School.*

Below right. Indian Club Drill at Dr Guthrie's Industrial School at Liberton in 1908. *Malcolm Cant Collection.*

❧ *Above*. The maypole was a popular attraction at Corstorphine Primary School at the opening of a school extension in 1910. The earliest record of a school in Corstorphine is 1646, established by George, the first Lord Forrester, in Albyn Cottage at the east end of the village. In 1819 a new school was built on the present site and extended in 1848, 1894 and 1910. On 12 September 1996 the school celebrated its 350th anniversary. *Malcolm Cant Collection.*

❧ *Above right*. All manner of costumes are in evidence for this day of pageantry at Donaldson's Hospital at West Coates, *c*. 1911. David Scott is between the boys in the back row. The building was designed by William H. Playfair and built by Young & Trench between 1842 and 1851. The Hospital was founded after the death, in 1830, of James Donaldson, publisher and printer of West Bow, who left the sum of £210,000 'to build and found an hospital for boys and girls to be called Donaldson's Hospital preferring those of the name Donaldson and Marshall'.
Courtesy of Mrs Sheila Bell, daughter of David Scott.

❧ *Right*. A distinctly seafaring theme was adopted by the pupils of Leith Academy Primary School for their mid-1930s school concert. The first Leith Academy in St Andrew Place in 1896 was confined to primary classes in 1931 when a new secondary school was built in Duke Street. *Courtesy of Mrs Mary Burnie, née McPhie.*

Left. The gymnastic display on the south-facing lawn at Esdaile College formed part of Moderator's Day in May 1937, when the Rt. Rev. Dugald MacFarlane visited the school. Founding an 'Educational Establishment for Clergymen's Daughters' in Kilgraston Road was the idea of two brothers, James and David Esdaile, whose father was the Rev. James Esdaile of Montrose. It was towards the end of his life that James discussed with his brother, David, the idea of founding the school. David Rhind was appointed architect and the school opened on 10 October 1863 with forty-two pupils. Although the school was opened for the daughters of ministers and university professors, this stipulation was relaxed in 1871 to include daughters of professional laymen where all vacancies had not been taken up. The school, renamed Esdaile College in 1926, celebrated its centenary in 1963, but closed in 1967. *Courtesy of Miss Molly Longmuir.*

Below left. A large group of children, and some adults, stretch across the roadway and perch on the railings at Roseburn Primary School in Roseburn Street. The school was designed in 1893 by the Edinburgh School Board architect, Robert Wilson, and opened the following year. The first headmaster received an annual salary of £290, plus free accommodation. *Malcolm Cant Collection.*

Below. The photograph shows a group of pupils and the headmaster, Andrew Myrtle Cockburn, on the right of the gate, at the schoolhouse in Morningside Road. Dating from 1823, it provided adequate accommodation for many years before the growth in Morningside's population in the late nineteenth century. Four eminent citizens were closely involved in its formation: George Ross of Woodburn House; Alexander Falconar of Falcon House; James Evans of Canaan Park; and Henry Hare of Newgrange. After the school closed in 1892 (when South Morningside School opened) the old building was taken over by the Christian Brethren. *Malcolm Cant Collection.*

Right. A class of fifty youngsters, 26 boys and 24 girls, well turned out with formal collars and strong footwear at Gilmore Place Public School in 1912. The girl in the second front row, fifth from the right, is Margaret Nelson. *Courtesy of Colin Dale.*

Below right. A group of boys and girls of mixed ages at the Misses Watt's Private School at No. 42 Liberton Brae, *c.* 1924. Those identified are all on the left of the picture: the 'shy' girl, on the extreme left of the picture, with the bow in her hair, is Helen Speedy who lived at No. 2 Liberton Brae. Next to her is Marjory White, a farmer's daughter from Edgefield, Loanhead. The blond girl, fourth from the left, is Jessie Nicolson of No. 12 Braefoot Terrace and the smaller girl to her left is Irene Swan of No. 8 Braefoot Terrace. The only other child definitely identified is the boy immediately behind Jessie and Irene: he is Kenneth Robertson who lived in Blackford Glen Road. *Courtesy of Miss E. M. Brodie.*

Below. An all-female group at Victoria School in Newhaven which has always been co-educational. Newhaven can trace the history of its schools to the early eighteenth century when the first recorded building was in School's Close or Lamb's Close, off Main Street. *Malcolm Cant Collection.*

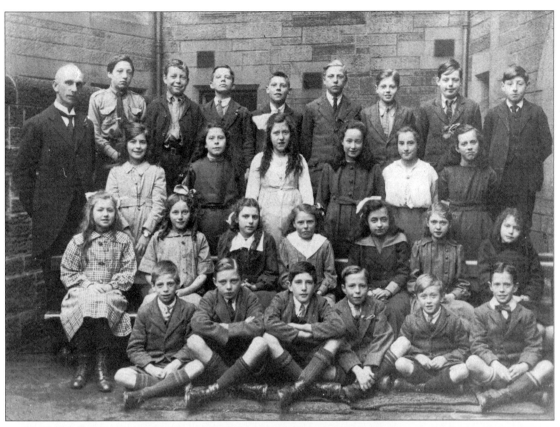

Left. An immaculately dressed teacher with a class of only 27 pupils at Warrender Park Board School in Marchmont Crescent in 1919. In 1882, the decision to build the school on that site was criticised on the grounds that the type of house in the district was intended for people who were unlikely to send their children to a Board school. In 1923 the school was renamed James Gillespie's Junior School and in 1929 it became James Gillespie's Boys' School. The last headmaster, Harold S. Wall, closed the school log on 10 September 1973. *Malcolm Cant Collection.*

Below. Almost all the pupils and staff of St Trinnean's School appear in this photograph taken in 1926 at St Leonard's House, off Dalkeith Road. St Trinnean's School for boarding and day pupils began in 1922 at No. 10 Palmerston Road under its only headmistress, Miss C. Fraser Lee. Her concept of the Dalton Plan for education, which allowed for a degree of choice on the part of the pupils, was revolutionary and attracted a great deal of attention, and criticism. The school remained at Palmerston Road until 1925 when it moved to St Leonard's House. At the outbreak of War in 1939 the school was evacuated to Galashiels but, owing to the retirement of Miss Lee, closed in September 1946. *Courtesy of Miss K. Sanderson.*

Right. H. M. Queen Elizabeth II visited The Edinburgh Academy at the time of the school's 150th anniversary. In this photograph, taken at Henderson Row on 5 July 1974, Her Majesty is accompanied by Dr H. H. Mills, M.C., the Rector at the time, and David Gregson, head ephor. The Edinburgh Academy was opened on 1 October 1824 under its first Rector, Dr John Williams, formerly of Winchester and of Lampeter College in Wales. The Academy building was designed by William Burn within a very modest budget of £13,000. *Courtesy of The Edinburgh Academy.*

Below right. A small boy, perhaps on his way to another school, perches on the wall to the left of the street orderly's cart and brush. He is obviously greatly taken by the display of semaphore being enacted by the Academy boys on the school playground, or Front Yards, as the area is known. The instructor can just be seen in front of the right-hand pillar, while the figure to his left appears to be the janitor, dressed in top hat and tails. *Courtesy of The Edinburgh Academy.*

Below. H. M. Queen Elizabeth II listens enthralled as Mark Blackadder explains how to glaze a pot. *Scotsman Publications Ltd.*

Left. The full complement of staff at Boroughmuir Senior Secondary School at the time of the fifty year anniversary in 1954. *Front row*, from left to right: J. W. Cassells; G. Iverach; G. Johnston; E. Anderson; E. D. Graham; S. McLean; U. A. Harris; J. Thorburn; R. L. S. Carswell (Headmaster); M. C. McGlashan; J. Fisher; W. A. Sandilands; W. Whitehead; M. J. Forsyth; J. C. Kidd; S. C. Ballantine. The first Boroughmuir School was in Warrender Park Crescent in the building which was later used as James Gillespie's High School for Girls. Classes began in September 1904 but the formal opening by the Rt. Hon. Charles Scott Dickson, K. C., M. P., Lord Advocate, was delayed until 3 February 1905. After his tour of the school the Lord Advocate stated that 'the most striking characteristic of every class is the high and perfectly uniform level of proficiency'. Boroughmuir vacated the Warrender Park Crescent building in 1914 and transferred to the new building in Viewforth where it has remained until the present day. *From* Boroughmuir Jubilee 1904–54.

Below left. The young graduate of Edinburgh University is Margaret Kinmont Ross, in April 1905, who went on to become principal of Craigmount School in Dick Place. Craigmount was first used as a boarding school for boys but in 1900 the buildings were taken over by the five Misses Gossip who ran it as a girls' school until their retirement in 1911. They were succeeded by Miss Macdonald and Mrs Henderson, then by the Misses Adamson, until Miss Margaret Kinmont Ross took over in 1932. The school was evacuated to Scone Palace in 1939 where it remained until 1952. It transferred to Minto House, near Hawick, and closed in 1966. When Craigmount was at Dick Place it occupied two main buildings on the south side of Dick Place where Wyvern Park now is. White House was nearest to Dick Place and Red House was due south: both buildings were by F. T. Pilkington who also designed Barclay Church. *Malcolm Cant Collection.*

Below right. William Bannerman, headmaster, and his wife, Agnes, outside the first Davidson's Mains School in Corbiehill Road in 1909. The school was opened in 1874, prior to which there were two other village schools: one was the Free Church School and the other was Lauriston School for Girls. The 1874 building was demolished in 1967 and replaced by a new school on the same site, opened by the Rt. Rev. R. Leonard Small. *Malcolm Cant Collection.*

❧ *Right*. Canongate Kirk Boys' Choir was founded in 1946: initially the boys wore purple cassocks which were later changed to scarlet 'as befitted a royal foundation'. On the right of the picture is the Rev. William Vernon Selby Wright, minister of Canongate Kirk from 1937 until 1978. The history of the Boys' Club and Choir, entitled *Our Club*, was published in 1954. *Photograph by Norward Inglis.*

❧ *Below right*. St Martin's Episcopal Church Male Choir in 1903. The Episcopal Church of St Martin of Tours was established in Gorgie in 1883 in a small mission building at White Park on the south side of Gorgie Road. The Rev. N. W. Usher, one of the chaplains from St Mary's Cathedral, was appointed in charge and early services were taken by Charles Pressley-Smith when he was still a divinity student. The first congregation consisted of one man and a few children. A permanent stone church was built at Murieston and the first service was held on 14 July 1900. After the building was demolished in 1983 because of subsidence, the congregation moved to the former Baptist Church building on the corner of Dalry Road and Murieston Crescent.

❧ *Below*. At Blackhall St Columba's Church in the late 1950s, the Rev. J. Watson Mathewson prepares to baptise the child of Moira and David Russell.

❧ *Above*. Thomas Buchan, church officer, standing at the doorway of Free St Paul's Church, St Leonard's Street, in 1894. The board on the right of the doorway states that Sabbath services were held at 11.00 a.m. and 2.30 p.m. and the Sabbath School was held at 4.00 p.m.
Courtesy of Miss Constance MacKenzie.

❧ *Above left*. The Rev. John (Jock) Richard Wilson shaking hands with members of his congregation at the door of St Brides Parish Church in Orwell Terrace. A few years after this photograph was taken, St Brides amalgamated with Dalry Haymarket Church to form St Colm's Parish Church in Dalry Road. The St Brides Church building became a community centre. *Malcolm Cant Collection.*

❧ *Left*. Blackhall St Columba's Church stands on the corner of Queensferry Road and Columba Road. It was designed by P. MacGregor Chalmers in 1903 and opened on 28 May 1904 although it was still unfinished. The photograph clearly shows that the intended octagonal spire on the north-west corner was never built. *Malcolm Cant Collection.*

❧ *Above.* A very historic occasion captured at the raising of the tenor bell at St Cuthbert's Parish Church in 1902. The bell, cast in Loughborough, bears the inscription 'James MacGregor D. D., and A. Wallace Williamson D. D., Ministers of St Cuthbert's 1901'. The two ministers are holding the rope: Dr MacGregor on the left and Dr Williamson on the right. Behind them, from left to right are: John MacDonald, caretaker (partly hidden); Mr Rankine, beadle; Mr Wood, beadle. In front, from left to right: Archibald Ballantine, artist; Mrs Wallace Williamson; and Hippolyte J. Blanc, architect. *Courtesy of Trevor Yerbury.*

❧ *Above right.* Laying the foundation stone of Greenbank United Free Church on 24 April 1926 by the Rev. James Harvey D. D., Moderator of the United Free Church. The church was designed by A. Lorne Campbell and built by William Gerard & Sons of Wheatfield Street. *Photograph by George Blyth Logie. Courtesy of Greenbank Parish Church.*

❧ *Right.* The children from the youth organisations of St Bride's Church in Dalry were photographed in 1933 at the studio of Thomson Bros., the photographers, in West Maitland Street. The children depict the various characters in the popular verse, *Tinker, Tailor, Soldier, Sailor.* Nan Allison is 'the tailor' seated on the right of the picture. *Courtesy of Mrs Nan Jamieson, née Allison.*

❧ *Left*. Two heavily laden barges ready to leave Stoneyport on the Union Canal, near Lanark Road. The children and adults are *en route* for Ratho on a Sunday School picnic from Colinton Parish Church. At one time, Stoneyport was a very busy loading point for stone cut from the nearby quarries of Hailes and Redhall. *Malcolm Cant Collection.*

❧ *Below left*. Several carts are lined up at the north end of Dreghorn Loan to take the children of Colinton Parish Church on their annual Sunday School picnic in 1909. There has been some form of ecclesiastical presence on the site of the present church since 1095. In 1771 a fairly substantial stone building was erected by Robert Weir and William Watters which was extended and improved by the architect, David Bryce, in 1837. When this photograph was taken, the church had only just completed a further major alteration to the building by the architect, Sydney Mitchell, in which the gables were rearranged and the square tower was rebuilt. *Malcolm Cant Collection.*

❧ *Below*. In this photograph the children are already having their picnic with Father John Shand at St Salvador's Episcopal Church at Stenhouse. The building was designed by the architects, Tarbolton & Ochterlony, the foundation stone was laid on 11 December 1937, and the church was opened in November 1938. *Courtesy of Mrs Sheila Miller.*

❧ *Right.* In 1940, this group of children had the complete freedom of the large garden at No. 52 Morningside Park which surrounded the manse for Morningside Parish Church. The garden also had a tennis court which was sometimes used by the boys, unofficially, for football or 7-aside rugby. During the Second World War the Sunday school picnics were also held in the manse garden, only once disrupted by an air raid siren which turned out to be a false alarm. The picture shows, from left to right: Derek Thomson; Ann Wood, daughter of the minister, the Rev. Frank Wood; Arthur Wood, son of the minister; unidentified; Irene Thomson, sister of Derek; and Julie Goldsmith.
Courtesy of Arthur Wood.

❧ *Below right.* One man, fifty women and at least the same number of handbags form an interesting group at Cairns Memorial Church, Gorgie Road, sometime prior to 1953. The women are about to embark on the annual Women's Guild outing. The only member positively identified is Mrs Jemima Scoular who is the tall lady in the centre of the picture (back row) standing in front of the window mullion. *Courtesy of Mrs Pat Scoular.*

❧ *Below.* Molly Kane and a group of children at Argyle Place Church Sunday School picnic to Davidson's Mains *c.* 1930. *Malcolm Cant Collection.*

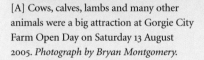

[A] Cows, calves, lambs and many other animals were a big attraction at Gorgie City Farm Open Day on Saturday 13 August 2005. *Photograph by Bryan Montgomery.*

[B] Young boys are never happier than when they are at the wheel of a tractor: Callum Gould at Gorgie City Farm on 2 June 2006. *Photograph by Phyllis M. Cant.*

[C] The Lochrin Basin and the Leamington Lift Bridge (renovated in 2002) were reopened on 22 March 2005 by the Minister for Transport, Nicol Stephen M.S.P. The children watching the first boat going through are from Tollcross Primary School. *Photograph by Bryan Montgomery.*

[D] On the same day, the pleasure craft, *Kelvin*, belonging to the Edinburgh Canal Society, makes its way towards the Lochrin Basin. *Photograph by Bryan Montgomery.*

[A]

[B]

[C]

[A] The illustration comes from an undated sales brochure packed with information and prices on Ladies' Wear, Gents' Wear, Boys' Wear, Girls' Dresses, Everything for the Outdoor Life, Furnishing Bargains and Wedding Gifts. Star Value was the Belvedere carriage-built pram at £3.12.6d.

[B] A single customer is being served at the Bristo Street premises by an experienced assistant and two younger assistants learning the trade. Sale prices, according to contemporary catalogues, included: Pure Silk Stockings reduced from 3/11d to 2/11d (15p).

[C] Another of Parkers' sales brochures assured customers that they could 'Order with complete confidence from Parkers, Satisfaction Guaranteed or money refunded'. The style of hat worn by the ladies came from a range 'Smart Hats in the Season's Newest Styles', all priced at 3/11d (20p).

[D] All manner of goods and prices are available in one of Parkers' busiest departments. A 1956 Home & Family Catalogue included a very wide selection of goods from Infants Wear: Useful & Dainty to Workaday Wear for men's blue denim overalls and boiler suits.
All courtesy of Pat and Tony Winkle.

[D]

[A] Helen and Bill Teviotdale behind the counter at the St Mary's Street branch of Caseys of Edinburgh in February 2006 shortly before the firm closed for business. The firm was established by Bill's uncle, James Casey. In 1925, when he was 15 years of age, James was apprenticed to the confectionery maker, Marwick's of Fountainbridge. When they went into liquidation in the late 1920s they were taken over by Mackays who operated from the same premises for many years, but James Casey was not kept on after he had completed his apprenticeship. He started his own business in the early 1930s in Potterrow when the family was living nearby at No. 13 Carnegie Street. His sisters, Cathy and Ellen, also assisted in the shop. Bill started full time with the firm in 1962 and Helen in 1970. *Photograph by Peter Stubbs.*

[B] Casey's premises at No. 52 St Mary's Street with the founder, James Casey, reading the *Evening News* which included articles on promoting small businesses. *Scotsman Publications Ltd.*

[C] Caseys have always been famous for a wide range of confectionery, most of it made on the premises at No. 52 St Mary's Street. The selection includes: Soor Plooms; Barley Sugar; Easter Road Rock; Cinnamon Balls; Raspberry Fizzies and many more. *Photograph by Peter Stubbs.*

[B]

[C]

[A] The pipes and drums of the Barnton Pipe Band played a selection of marches, strathspeys and reels in Murieston Park at the Gorgie Dalry Gala Day on Saturday 10 June 2006. *Photograph by Bryan Montgomery.*

[B] The Household Cavalry are as photogenic as ever as they leave Redford Barracks on their way to official engagements during the visit to Edinburgh of the King and Queen of Norway in 1994. *Malcolm Cant Collection.*

[C] An armoured vehicle, suitably camouflaged, turns onto Waverley Bridge at the rear of the last parade of the Royal Scots on Friday 26 May 2006 before becoming part of the new Royal Regiment of Scotland. *Malcolm Cant Collection.*

[A]

[B]

[C]

64

PART 3: AT WORK AND ON PARADE

Part 3 has 80 photographs, the larger portion of which illustrates different aspects of employment. These range from fairly heavy industries like engineering and boat-building to the much lighter service industries of hairdressers and office workers. The section opens with two occupations which have not disappeared altogether but are radically different to what they were when the photographs were taken. In fact it might be said that one of them, bill-posting, is now so prolific that an increased number of street orderlies, or cleansing staff, are required to curtail its worst excesses.

Like any other comparable city, Edinburgh has grown over the years to encompass more and more peripheral farmland. That development, in which many people were required to alter their lifestyles, has been recorded in photographs at Braid, Greenbank, Liberton and Davidson's Mains. The heavy industries are represented by Mathers the engineers who were at Dalry, Ramage & Ferguson, the famous shipbuilders of Leith, and the smaller firm of Allan & Brown at Newhaven. Other firms of national significance were Colin C. Macandrew & Partners who built Redford Barracks, and Scott Morton & Co., who supplied the craftsmen for the Thistle Chapel at St Giles Cathedral. Smaller, one-man firms included Alexander Dobson, the slater, who worked on the City Poorhouse at Glenlockhart, and William Scoular, the coal merchant, followed

by his son, Archibald, who ensured that the Gorgie and Dalry home fires were kept burning.

At one time female employees tended to be confined to specific occupations more so than they are nowadays. Those included in this section are 'the girls' from McVitie & Price, the biscuit manufacturers, a comptometer operator at Ramage & Ferguson, several groups of nurses, and, of course, the fishwives of Newhaven.

There are several transport-related pictures, the motive power including the humble horse,

Above. The country bill-poster, photographed on the outskirts of Edinburgh, looks relatively relaxed on his rounds, complete with canister of paste, long-handled brush and a supply of advertisements. *Courtesy of Miss Constance MacKenzie.*

Opposite. Alexander Hoy served in the Royal Scots during the First World War after which he took a job as a street orderly, or 'scaffie', as they were known in Edinburgh at that time. He is seen here with brush, shovel and barrow in Chesser Avenue, c. 1920. *Courtesy of May Hoy.*

Hospital in the 1940s. The lighter side of work and employment includes the staff of the Buttercup Dairy Company preparing for a pageant and the North British Rubber Company staff, winners of a skittles cup enjoying their success. The work-related photographs conclude with a selection pertaining to the Edinburgh photographer, Norward Inglis, whose work appears in several parts of this book.

The second, smaller section of Part 3 relates to parades and ceremonies which include the Royal Proclamation of Queen Elizabeth II at the Mercat Cross, the official opening of the Edinburgh Festival in 1949, and the laying of the foundation stone at St David's Church in Viewforth. The various youth organisations are included, the Boys' Brigade, the Boy Scouts and the Brownies, as well as the Territorial Army. Other military pictures include: the Scots Guards passing St Andrew's House on 24 June 1953 as part of the ceremonial state drive to mark the Coronation of Queen Elizabeth II; and the combined military and pipe bands of the Royal Scots outside Bruntsfield School in 1918. To complete the book, there are pictures of the March of the 1000 pipers along Princes Street in 1951; the North British Rubber Company Pipe Band returning to Castle Mills after an engagement; and the last parade of the Royal Scots before becoming part of the new Royal Regiment of Scotland.

steam, electricity and the petrol and diesel engine. Horse-drawn vehicles, mostly for hire, are pictured on Princes Street and other locations. The steam-driven transport includes a Stanley 10-h.p. Roadster and Macandrew's 'pug' which pulled building materials from Slateford Road to Redford Barracks. Others include an early tour bus or charabanc, and Player's taxi fleet from the 1950s. Several views of tram cars are included, the most nostalgic being those showing the crew either resting at the terminus or preparing the

tram for the return journey.

The three main emergency services, fire, police and ambulance, are also included to which has been added the hospital service. Police officers on duty, formal groups and police inspections are followed by an array of fire-fighting equipment at Lauriston, Abbeyhill and Stockbridge. The hospital selection has at least two very poignant pictures: First World War casualties at St Raphael's Hospital in the Grange, and the boys' ward at the Princess Margaret Rose

Right. The photograph was taken in 1910 by the Edinburgh photographer, R. A. Rayner, in what is now Braidburn Valley Park. At that time it was part of Greenbank Farm which included all of the ground on which the bungalows of Greenbank were built in the 1930s. In the photograph, the small thatched cottage with the central chimney near the left of the picture, was used by farm workers. The next building, which is fitted with iron bars across the windows, is a temporary site hut for David Adamson of Morningside Road who is in the process of completing Nos. 1-7 Greenbank Crescent. The people working on the stooks of corn probably include members of the Moggie family who were one of the last tenant farmers at Greenbank. *Malcolm Cant Collection.*

Below right. Janet and Daniel Moggie came to Greenbank Farmhouse as tenant farmers towards the end of the nineteenth century where they brought up ten children. In 1926 they retired to Millar Crescent. *Courtesy of Lynne Common and Elizabeth Butchart, great-granddaughters.*

Below. Three farmers at Braid Farm, *c.* 1924. From left to right: Duncan Campbell of Woodhall Farm, Juniper Green; William Wilkie of Braid Farm and Comiston Farm; and Sandy Campbell of Corstorphine Bank Farm. William Wilkie and his wife Barbara came from Fife to Braid Farm in 1916 and also took over responsibility for Comiston Farm from 1925 until 1937. *Courtesy of Miss Isla Wilkie.*

❧ *Left.* Bringing in the sheaves at Little Road with Liberton Gardens in the background, 1949. Little Road was named in 1931 from the Little family, owners of a large part of the district from the time of William Litil (Little) who was Lord Provost of Edinburgh from 1586-87 and again for a year in 1591. *Courtesy of Mr & Mrs Philp.*

❧ *Below left.* One of the smiddies in Davidson's Mains was run by John Macdonald, horseshoer and general blacksmith, at the east end of the village. Davidson's Mains was known as Muttonhole until about 1850 but there is doubt about the derivation of the name which is recorded at least as early as 1669. One theory suggests a hollow in which sheep were slaughtered which would certainly fit in with the rural character of the district before it became part of the City of Edinburgh. *Courtesy of Mrs Sadie Fraser.*

❧ *Below.* Mrs Margaret Scott and her daughter, Violet, at Greenbank Farmhouse, *c.* 1923. Mrs Scott was housekeeper to Dick Boa the last tenant farmer who also had a dairy at Dorset Place. When the bungalows of Greenbank were being built in the 1930s, the farmhouse was not demolished immediately as it was hoped that it could be renovated to form part of the new district. However, nothing came of the idea and it was demolished in 1934. *Courtesy of Mrs Violet Gordon, née Scott.*

Right. The workforce of Colin Macandrew & Partners Ltd., Public Works Contractors, at West End Place in the mid-1930s. A siding from the Caledonian Railway gave access to the yard for bringing in materials and taking away finished work. Prior to the First World War, Macandrew was the main contractor on several important public buildings in Edinburgh, including Redford Barracks. Before work was started, a light railway was built from Slateford station to Colinton Road to transport the vast quantities of materials required for the job. Perhaps the most prestigious of all the contracts, however, was for the construction of the National Library of Scotland on George IV Bridge, designed in 1934 but delayed by the Second World War and not completed until 1955. In the photograph, the only person identified is Archibald Cunningham Robson who is second from the right in the back row. *Courtesy of Phyllis M. Cant, née Robson.*

Below right. The staff of Scott Morton, Joiners and Cabinetmakers, from Murieston are obviously having a day away from the work benches to participate in the Royal Infirmary pageant passing down Lothian Road. On the back of the lorry, the staff are believed to be re-enacting the story of Grizel Baillie (1665-1746) who is trying to bar the door against entry by the political enemies of her father, Sir Patrick Hume. *Photograph by Frank Wilson.*

Below. William Scoular, Snr, the coal merchant, in Duff Street Lane, *c.* 1930, where he stabled his two Clydesdale horses which took it in turn to haul the fully laden cart through the streets of Gorgie and Dalry. After William died in 1940, his son, Archibald, continued the business but invested in a Fordson lorry. *Courtesy of Pat & Douglas Scoular.*

Left. Slaters hard at work preparing slates for the roof of Edinburgh City Poorhouse (now redeveloped as part of the Steils, off Glenlockhart Road). The Poorhouse was built by William Beattie between 1867-70. The man in the centre of the picture is Alexander Dobson Snr, whose photograph, on his fortieth wedding anniversary, appears on page 21. *Courtesy of Mrs Pauline Matthews.*

Below left. This group of workers, *c.* 1930, which includes two ladies with collecting cans, was employed by the Buttercup Dairy Company whose premises lay between the east side of Easter Road and the bottom of Lochend Road. The location is confirmed by the position of Lochend Road School and the spire of Leith St Andrew's Church on the left. The central attraction seems to be the cockerel and the small traction vehicle with the sign 'Buttercup Poultry Farm'. If the larger signs says: 'Feed the Caterpillar, throw in Your Cash', then the event may have been associated with the Leith Pageant which raised money for good causes. *Courtesy of Linda Pittilo, née Anderson.*

Below. Archibald Scoular, coal merchant, son of William Scoular, Snr, with his 1948 Bedford lorry, *c.* 1950. The vehicle was purchased from Scottish Motor Traction Co., of Roseburn Street. In the days when almost every household in Gorgie and Dalry had coal-burning grates, Archibald had almost 3,000 customers. At nearby Gorgie East sidings, each coal merchant had his own lye where he would fill hundred-weight bags directly from the railway wagons coming in from the Klondyke pit at Newcraighall. Thereafter, came the even more arduous task of delivering the coal to all the tenement flats, many of them on the top floor. *Courtesy of Pat & Douglas Scoular.*

❧ *Above.* The Orwell Works of Alexander Mather & Son in Orwell Terrace was a hive of activity with lathes, an overhead gantry crane and a light railway all competing for space when this photograph was taken in 1921. The main contracts, firstly at Fountainbridge and later Orwell Terrace, were for the construction and supply of oatmeal and barley milling machines, conveyor and elevator equipment, cutting and stacking machines for paper mills, and printing ink manufacturing plant.

❧ *Above right.* In 1870, long before the internal combustion engine became commonplace, Mather's designed and built a steam-powered tractor which was on show at the International Exhibition of Industry, Science and Art held in the East Meadows in the summer of 1886. It was not an agricultural tractor intended to be used in the fields but was designed to pull heavy loads on a reasonably firm surface. As can be seen from the illustration, it was a short, stocky, three-wheeled vehicle with massive rear wheels supporting the steam boiler and funnel. Two men were required to operate it: the driver sat perched at the front in an open cab, while a second person was stationed on a projecting platform at the back, presumably to stoke the boiler.

❧ *Right.* This group of eleven working men was employed by Ramage & Ferguson, the Leith shipbuilders in the early 1920s. The firm built 296 vessels of various types during the 56 years of the yard's existence. Henry Robb started as yard manager before the First World War and during 1918 started in business under his own name. In 1933 his former yard, Ramage & Ferguson, ceased trading and Henry Robb Ltd. gained full control of the Victoria Shipyard. Nowadays, the new shopping complex, Ocean Terminal, occupies the site of the slipways of the former yard. In the photograph, the man on the left, in a row by himself, is David Anderson. *Courtesy of Linda Pittilo, née Anderson.*

Left. The staff on the roof of the Santou Hairdressing Salon in the 1920s at No. 85 Shandwick Place, with Frances Deuchars, front row, extreme right. *Photograph by Frank Wilson.*

Below left. In 1909, prior to the First World War, the Government set up the Volunteer Aid Detachment organised by the British Red Cross Society and others, with basic training in first aid and home nursing. However, these ladies do not appear to be part of the VAD as they do not have the characteristic Red Cross on the front of their uniforms. In the photograph the lady standing on the right is Ena Leask and her sister, Sarah, is sitting in front of her. *Courtesy of Linda Pittilo, née Anderson.*

Below centre. This young lady is all dressed up ready for collecting on behalf of the Royal Infirmary of Edinburgh. At the time of the Royal Infirmary Pageant held in Edinburgh on 26 May 1923, the hospital issued picture postcards as mementoes giving some important facts and figures. Patients treated in the year ending 1 October 1922 numbered 14,156 and there was a deficit of £20,587 between income and expenditure. *Malcolm Cant Collection.*

Below. Ena Leask, comptometer operator with Ramage & Ferguson, the Leith shipbuilders, in 1925, several years after working as a volunteer nurse. *Courtesy of Linda Pittilo, née Anderson.*

❧ *Above.* Wha'll buy my caller herrin? Two fisherwomen, complete with creels, pass the time of day on their rounds in the Trinity area of the City. © *Edinburgh City Libraries. *

❧ *Above right.* The last boat made at Newhaven, *Reliance*, built at Allan & Brown's yard at Fishermen's Park in 1929, is hauled through the streets of Newhaven to the harbour. Newhaven's boat-building history goes back many years to the sixteenth century when the *Great Michael* was launched in 1511 as the largest ship then afloat. Designed by the famous naval architect, Jacques Tarette, to be the flagship of the Scottish navy, it required for its construction all the oak in Fife save that at Falkland Palace. *Courtesy of the Carnie family.*

❧ *Right.* Members of the Newhaven Fisherwomen's Choir photographed in their Gala costumes in the late 1930s. The choir celebrated its Golden Jubilee in 1977 when a commemorative seat was presented, at the foot of Craighall Road, by Charles Addison, but unfortunately the choir ceased a few years later. The other local choir was the Newhaven Fisher Girls' Choir, established in 1889, which later changed its name to Newhaven Fisher Lassies' Choir. It continued until 1995 under its conductor, Robert Allan, who had led the choir since 1938. *Malcolm Cant Collection.*

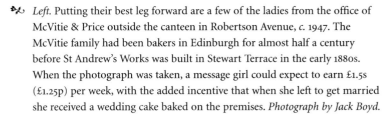

Left. Putting their best leg forward are a few of the ladies from the office of McVitie & Price outside the canteen in Robertson Avenue, *c.* 1947. The McVitie family had been bakers in Edinburgh for almost half a century before St Andrew's Works was built in Stewart Terrace in the early 1880s. When the photograph was taken, a message girl could expect to earn £1.5s (£1.25p) per week, with the added incentive that when she left to get married she received a wedding cake baked on the premises. *Photograph by Jack Boyd.*

Below left. Time for a quick celebratory drink by the winning team from the North British Rubber Company, later Uniroyal, in the early 1960s. The photograph was taken in the Sports and Social Club premises of Alexanders of Edinburgh at Rosemount Lane, near Gardner's Crescent. Third from the left is Dave Browne who is touching the arm of Ken Alexander. Tommy Finerty is drinking from the cup, to the right of which is Ben Brodie with his hands crossed. Jack Boyd, with a cigarette in his left hand, is to the right of the man with the blazer badge. *Courtesy of Jack Boyd.*

Below. Councillor Betty Mackenzie at McLeod Street Public Washhouse, *c.* 1980. In 1981 the building was converted to McLeod Street Leisure Centre. *Courtesy of Mrs Betty Mackenzie.*

Right. This small railway engine, or pug, Andrew Barclay 1223, belonged to Colin Macandrew & Partners, Public Works Contractors, of West End Place, off Dalry Road. It was used on a short private railway line between Slateford Station and Colinton Road to convey the vast amount of stone, timber and other materials used in the construction of Redford Barracks which began in 1909. The photograph was taken on 15 May 1959 at N. Greening & Sons Ltd. Works at Warrington, and now operates at the Chasewater Pleasure Park, Brownhills, West Midlands.
Courtesy of Mrs S. Peden.

Below. William Hay Hunter, founder of the firm W. H. Hunter (Motors) Ltd., inspecting a 1912 Stanley 10-h.p. Roadster at the firm's Braid Road premises, *c.* 1950. The steam-driven car is still in the possession of the Hunter family and is frequently used on the road at rallies and other events. W. H. Hunter (Motors) Ltd. can trace their association with the motor trade back to its infancy at the beginning of the twentieth century. The firm was established in 1919 by William Hay Hunter who served his apprenticeship with Robert Wight Jnr, Automobile Engineers, of East Newington Place before opening his own business in Balcarres Street in 1919. The firm moved to purpose-built premises in Braid Road in 1922 where William Hay Hunter's son, Bill, joined the business in 1946, and grandson, Alistair, in 1984. The firm closed in 1997. *Courtesy of Bill Hunter.*

Below right. Edinburgh Corporation Transport 'charabanc' Leyland B8725, complete with solid tyres, running boards and hood, in West Mains Road, 1919, near the present-day Scottish headquarters of the British Geological Survey, with Arthur's Seat in the background.
Photograph by E. O. Catford.

❧ *Above*. An open-topped double-decker bus with solid tyres, at an unknown location, with the driver, John Alexander Segger, on the right, *c*. 1925. The identity of the conductor has not been established. *Courtesy of Alex Segger.*

❧ *Above left*. In the 1950s, this elderly gentleman still maintained a strong link with earlier, more elegant, forms of transport. The carriage appears to be a landau with twin hoods which could be closed over the passenger compartment during inclement weather. Its position on Princes Street near the steps to the Waverley Station made it a much sought after stance. *Photograph by Norward Inglis.*

❧ *Left*. This row of elegant Dodge taxis was photographed in 1936 at the west entrance to the Royal Botanic Garden by Violet Banks, a professional photographer, of No. 21 Charlotte Square. The consecutive registration numbers, ASC 346 to ASC 354 (ASC 352 does not appear in the photograph) were issued, *en bloc*, in November or December 1936, over the counter, at the Local Taxation Office in the High Street. The numbers were allocated to John Player's fleet of blue taxis which operated from the company's garage premises at No. 71 Pitt Street which was merged with Dundas Street in 1967. In 1948, Player's business was acquired by Electrobat Services Ltd., who sold off the taxi fleet in 1951. The same premises were used by Ford Dealers, Alexanders of Edinburgh from 1954 until 1979. *Courtesy of Douglas A. Glass.*

Right. Car 218 on service No. 12 leaving the island stop at the West End, *en route* for Corstorphine on 13 June 1954. The advertisement is for Burnett's White Satin Gin. The car looks as though it is full up as the regulator (with the white cap), and some of the passengers, are looking towards Princes Street for the next tram. It is difficult to say if the man with the golf bag is crossing the road or trying to jump the queue! *Photograph by George Fairley.*

Below. A different car, but the same route, with the driver, George Graham, giving a smart salute as he approaches the Zoo at high speed on 11 October 1953. This time the advertisement is for Dexter Weatherproofs. *Photograph by George Fairley.*

Below right. On a warm summer day, on 8 August 1953, the crew (James Paterson, conductor and George Graham, driver) has a well-earned rest from their labours at the Maybury terminus before setting off back to town, and then on to Joppa. The supplementary destination board at the front of the tram says: 'To & from Portobello Beach & Pool'. At the terminus the crewmen would normally have time 'to have their piece' or sandwiches, with or without the luxury of 'Luxor Sauce: Good with every meal' as recommended on the side of the tram. On the right-hand side of the picture the Maybury Roadhouse is advertising 'Restaurant: Dancing'. *Photograph by George Fairley.*

Left. Car 266 on service No. 11, bound for Stanley Road, is waiting at the Fairmilehead terminus on 11 September 1954. The advertisement on the side of the tram is for Weston's Quality Biscuits 'Save Pence Per Pound'. The conductor's arm is raised because he is pulling down on the rope attached to the overhead trolley, ready to place it on the wire above. The 'skate', seen above the trolley, was installed at all terminii and other important crossovers in 1940 to assist conductors to locate the wire, especially when it was dark. A group of people is heading to board the tram, probably having visited patients in the Princess Margaret Rose Hospital in Frogston Road West. *Photograph by George Fairley.*

Below left. The advertisement says: 'Grant's Guaranteed Furniture Lasts a Lifetime', but apparently tram cars do not. These two gentlemen have brought car No. 307 to the end of the line in North Junction Street on 2 August 1954 from where it will be jacked up onto the scrap merchant's lorry. *Photograph by M. J. Robertson. Courtesy of George Fairley.*

Below. Car No. 200, with no service number, photographed at Linkfield Road on 12 April 1954 as the conductor is repositioning the trolley. The car has brought spectators to a race meeting at Musselburgh and is about to return to the depot at Bath Street, Portobello. *Photograph by George Fairley.*

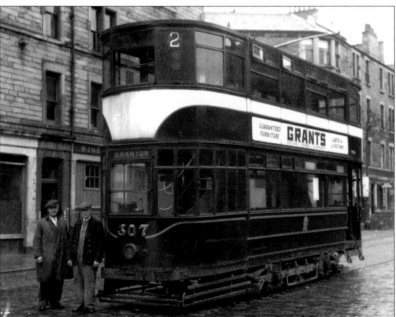

Right. A solitary police constable stands guard at important works on Slateford Road at the bottom of Craiglockhart Avenue. The original stone bridge, with a very narrow arch, which carried the Union Canal over the roadway, has been completely removed. A single pipe has been installed temporarily to maintain the water supply towards Meggetland and Fountainbridge. The new, single-arch concrete bridge, which is still in existence, carries the date 1937. *Photograph by Frank Wilson.*

Below. Changing shifts on points duty at the junction of Salisbury Road and Minto Street in the early 1930s. On the left is P. C. Alexander Norrie, and, on the right, P. C. John Kennell. *Courtesy of Mrs Helen Davidson.*

Below right. At the outbreak of the Second World War, the Edinburgh Special Constables paraded on the Castle Esplanade for their annual inspection. In the background is the turreted memorial to the soldiers of the Gordon Highlanders who died in the South African War, 1899-1902. Counting from the right-hand turret of the memorial, the third Special Constable is Archibald McInnes. In the early days, the Special Constables wore arm bands and carried truncheons bearing the City coat-of-arms. At the present day there are about 150 Special Constables who have the same uniform and powers of arrest as a regular officer. *Courtesy of Mrs Betty Styles, née McInnes.*

Left. The policeman on points duty at the junction of Castle Street and Princes Street would normally do a two-hour stint, followed by a similar period on patrol, and so on until the end of his shift. All the Princes Street junctions, except the West End, were manned from Gayfield Square Police Station, but the West End, and usually South Charlotte Street, were manned from West End Police Station in Torphichen Place. Traffic lights along the entire length of Princes Street were introduced in 1972. A regulation changing police uniform from helmets to flat hats was passed in 1950 but it took several months for it to be fully implemented. *Photograph by Norward Inglis.*

Below left. This group of Edinburgh policemen, photographed some time between 1919 and 1932, all appear to be attached to B Division at Gayfield Square. They are wearing ceremonial uniform with helmet spikes and ornamental chin straps which sit round the peak of the helmet. From left to right their collar numbers appear to be: *back row,* B266, B302, B259, B316, B279; *front row,* B284, B267, B319. *Malcolm Cant Collection.*

Below. This large complement of officers is the Leith Police Annual Inspection of 1910. A patent, dated 1908, altered the design of the helmets to include a 'ball' top but this does not yet appear to have been implemented.
Malcolm Cant Collection.

Right. Outside Clark's Bar at No. 80 Lauriston Place, the bar staff, a few regulars and some children are fascinated by the horse-drawn fire engine returning to the Central Fire Station at the head of Lady Lawson Street. The cloud of steam is not coming from the horses but from the water pump at the back of the tender. David Clark also ran the Cattle Market Hotel from No. 80 Lauriston Place, the name being taken from the nearby market and slaughterhouse. *Courtesy of Pat Scoular.*

Below. This two-horse fire tender is standing outside one of Edinburgh's small district fire units, London Road Fire Station, which was at Nos. 26 & 27 East Norton Place. The ground floor of the building was converted into retail outlets many years ago. The identity of the firemen in the photograph has not been established but may have included the young man (or his colleagues) who wrote the original postcard in 1907 to a friend, S. H. Sullens, Fire Station, Mile End Road, London E. His signature is indecipherable but he says: 'I was very busy last week going through my final exam for the maximum pay'. *Malcolm Cant Collection.*

Below right. Stockbridge fire brigade, in formal pose, seen outside the station in Hamilton Place, *c.* 1900, when brass helmets, buttons and accoutrements were the order of the day. The actual fire-fighting equipment was, however, rather rudimentary and not very speedy. *Courtesy of Lothian & Borders Fire Brigade.*

Left. A large crowd has gathered at the junction of St Stephen Street and North West Circus Place to watch the local fire brigade tackle a blaze above the premises of Alexander Breck, the hatter, at No. 4 Baker's Place, and Robert Bowie, the licensed grocer, at No. 5 (below the ladder) in 1901. The fire was a very extensive one which originated in Todd's Flour Mill to the rear of Baker's Place. Several people lost their lives and many others were injured. At the present day, Baker's Place forms part of Kerr Street. The tenement buildings on the west side of Kerr Street were demolished, probably needlessly, many years ago. *Courtesy of Lothian & Borders Fire Brigade.*

Below left. A full complement of firemen, of various ranks, pose with the very latest mechanised tender belonging to Edinburgh Fire Brigade. The undated photograph was taken at the Central Fire Station at Lauriston Place. *Malcolm Cant Collection.*

Below. The Central Fire Station in Lauriston Place was built between 1897 and 1901 to designs by the City Architect, Robert Morham, using pale green slates from Cumberland for the roof. Its red sandstone exterior was dutifully followed by the adjacent College of Art in 1906, and, almost a century later by Novotel Edinburgh on the corner of Lady Lawson Street. The characteristic tall square tower with the open top was used for drying hoses. To the rear of the main building there was also a tenement 'shell' used for fire-fighting practice using extending ladders, hoists and body slings. The Fire Station was built on the site of one of the City's slaughterhouse and cattle market which extended northwards almost as far as the West Port. When the new Fire Station was built at Tollcross, the old Lauriston building became a museum housing old tenders, fire-fighting equipment and the records of the many fires in Edinburgh over the years. *Malcolm Cant Collection.*

Right. The photograph shows the Community of the Little Company of Mary in 1950 at the entrance to the 1934 extension to St Raphael's Hospital on the corner of South Oswald Road and Blackford Avenue. The building in which St Raphael's was based was built in the late 1870s for Hugh Rose Jnr, the eldest son of Hugh Rose the founder of the paint firm, Craig & Rose, of Leith. The house, designed by David MacGibbon, was named Kilravock after Kilravock Castle near Nairn, the seat of the Rose clan. At the end of the First World War, Kilravock was acquired by the Scottish Branch of the British Red Cross and Ministry of Pensions to be converted into a house for severely disabled ex-servicemen. The project was organised by a committee under the direction of Lady Anne Kerr, sister of the Duke of Norfolk, who invited the Little Company of Mary to make preparations to receive the first patients. The house was opened in 1919 under its new name, St Raphael's, after St Raphael the Angel of Healing, and in commemoration of Lady Anne's husband, Major-General Lord Ralph Kerr, who was killed in action in 1916. The Little Company of Mary opened the first female ward in 1929, built an extension in 1934, and embarked on a major rebuilding programme in 1965. In 1982, St Raphael's ceased to be a small general hospital for women. St Raphael's Housing Association Ltd. was formed to take over the hospital and to convert it to a nursing home. In 1989 the old name, Kilravock, was revived as a sheltered housing development to the north of the old house. *Courtesy of the Little Company of Mary.*

Below right. This rather poignant photograph shows a group of patients and staff at the doorway of St Raphael's Hospital, originally Kilravock, probably shortly after the end of the First World War. The hospital, staffed by six sisters, received its first patients in 1919 – thirty-three casualties from the battlefields of Europe, the first patient being a thirty-one year-old officer, described rather ambiguously in the hospital journal as a 'paralysed and incurable Protestant'. Despite the traumatic circumstances, a relatively cheerful atmosphere was maintained between the patients and the staff. The last First World War patient died at the hospital in 1958 almost forty years after the first admissions. *Courtesy of the Little Company of Mary.*

84

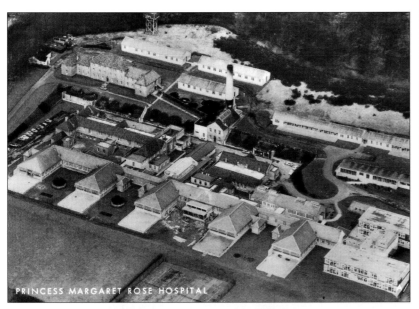

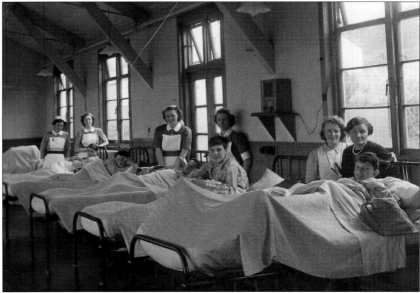

Above. The boys' ward of the Princess Margaret Rose Hospital, *c.* 1950. From left to right: Staff-nurse Noela Burton from New Zealand; Nurse Fitzgerald; Nurse Millan; Nurse Pullar; the maid, Jessie, from Ireland; and Miss Murdoch, a teacher. The patient on the extreme right is ten-year-old Alan Brotchie. The radio on the wall-shelf was put on for school programmes at regulated times only. *Courtesy of A. W. Brotchie.*

Above left. The Princess Margaret Rose Hospital in Frogston Road West was opened in 1929 as a children's orthopaedic hospital, but was later used for adults also. The aerial photograph shows the five pavilion-style wards, designed by the architect, Reginald Fairlie. In the left-hand corner of the picture, the Nurses Home is the long detached building of three storeys in the centre. To the right of it, the building with the chimney stack is the hospital laundry. Later additions to the original plans include the light-coloured glazed buildings in the bottom right-hand corner of the picture. The Princess Margaret Rose Hospital was closed in 2002 and most of the buildings (excluding the Nurses Home) were demolished for the construction of houses. © *Simmons Aerofilms Ltd.*

Left. George Honeyman, born at Cupar Muir, in Fife, in 1870, worked on the construction of the Forth Railway Bridge before taking a job with George Donaldson & Son, Wine & Spirit Merchants of West Maitland Street. He became an ambulance attendant at the City Hospital and was invited to the opening ceremony on Wednesday 13 May 1903. He is photographed here with one of the nurses at the City Hospital, *c.* 1920. *Courtesy of Mrs Elsie Burnie.*

❧ *Above left.* Norward Taylor Inglis, the professional photographer, dressed in formal attire, poses casually for the camera at an unknown location in the mid-1950s. Norward was born on 4 June 1921 in Stockbridge to Chilton Inglis, a dentist, and Jean Inglis, née Taylor, from Elgin. After schooling at The Edinburgh Academy, Norward worked as a clerk in the Salvesen Shipping Company in Leith, and then joined the R.A.F. as a photographer. He married Gladys Goalen in 1940. Following a brief business partnership in the mid-1940s he moved to No. 18 Regent Terrace where he continued in business on his own account for many years until partial retirement in 1965. *Courtesy of Barbara Simpson.*

❧ *Above right.* This Inglis family photograph was taken *c.* 1928 but the location has not been identified. Norward Inglis is sitting on the grass with Billy, the dog, on one side and a cousin, Elizabeth, on the other side. Norward's elder brother, Chilton, is standing at the back. On the reverse of the family photograph, the elderly lady is named only as 'Wee Grandma'. *Courtesy of Barbara Simpson.*

❧ *Right.* No. 18 Regent Terrace, *c.* 1950. The Terrace, originally built in 1826 with two storeys plus basement, has ornamental balconies and Doric pillars at the entrances. During ownership by the Inglis family, No. 18 was the family home and the place of business: the basement contained a workroom for retouching and trimming prints, a processing room, and a storage room in what had been the old kitchen; the ground floor contained the studio and an enlarging room; the first floor had a large lounge, which extended the full width of the property, with interconnecting doors to the dining room, and a kitchen; and the top floor had four bedrooms and a bathroom. Norward Inglis' car, which was used to carry his bulky photographic equipment, is parked outside. *Photograph by Norward Inglis.*

❧ *Above left.* Norward Inglis Film Productions was an integral part of the family business. The Arriflex camera is being operated by Mr Inglis who undertook several commissions for clients throughout the country, particularly in Edinburgh (including a film of the last tram in 1956) and in the north of Scotland. One of his earliest film commissions was a television advertisement for a Scottish Agricultural Industry fertiliser which was filmed in the Scottish Borders. He also took newsreel footage for the BBC which was then put on the train to Glasgow to be shown on the Scottish news later that evening. *Courtesy of Barbara Simpson.*

❧ *Above.* The studio at No. 18 Regent Terrace was at the front of the building on the ground floor. Shortly after this photograph was taken in 1955, a small hole was cut in the wall through to the adjacent enlarging room. The projector was placed in the enlarging room which reduced the noise when showing films in the studio, and also gave extra length between the projector and the screen. The studio was also used for receiving business visitors and setting out photographic displays. *Photograph by Norward Inglis.*

❧ *Left.* Despite the location, on a Princes Street rooftop, both participants, Joan Bakewell and Norward Inglis, have not yet reached the height of their careers.
Photograph by Kelly Photographer, South Queensferry.

Right. With absolute precision, and with assistance of the masons, the foundation stone for St David's Church in Viewforth is laid by Lord Glenconner, Lord High Commissioner, on 27 May 1911. St David's could trace its roots back to 1831 when Gardner's Hall Church, in Gardner's Crescent, was acquired. At the Disruption in 1843, St David's lost most of its congregation to the Free Church but later acquired land at Viewforth from the North British Rubber Company on which to build a larger church. Unfortunately, the completed building was never really seen to best advantage as it was designed to sit at right angles to Viewforth, the idea being that it would face onto a new street to be built between Viewforth and Gibson Terrace. When the new street was never built, the church was left with its main entrance facing onto a narrow passageway. *Malcolm Cant Collection.*

Below right. The officials and their wives were also photographed immediately after the ceremony of laying the foundation stone at St David's. The minister in the centre of the front row, holding the presentation mallet, is the Rev. W. R. Black, minister of St David's. *Malcolm Cant Collection.*

Below. In accordance with the custom of the time, a glass casket was placed in the foundations of St David's Church. When the building was demolished after the amalgamation of St David's and Viewforth St Oswald's in 1973, the casket was found and the contents recovered. Among them were these communion tokens and coins of the realm. *Malcolm Cant Collection.*

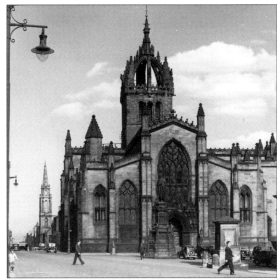

Top left. Some of the crowd and many of the camera crews are perched in precarious positions to witness a very historical moment at the Mercat Cross in the High Street. The occasion is the Royal Proclamation on 8 February 1952 of the accession to the throne of Queen Elizabeth II following the death of her father, King George VI, at Sandringham House on 6 February 1952. The Proclamation was read, firstly, by Lord Provost Sir James Miller, to the citizens of Edinburgh, and then by the Lord Lyon to the people of the Kingdom of Scotland.
Photograph by Norward Inglis.

Left. At the 1949 Edinburgh International Festival the customary Service of Praise was held at St Giles Cathedral after which the dignitaries walked in procession down the Royal Mile to the Palace forecourt. The opening ceremony included an invitation to speak by the Mayors and Burgomasters from many foreign cities. The photograph shows the representative from Athens.
Photograph by Norward Inglis.

Above. St Giles Cathedral on a quiet afternoon in the early 1950s. A few cars are parked indiscriminately to suit the convenience of the owners – much the same as they are nowadays. *Photograph by Norward Inglis.*

❧ *Right.* Brown Owl, May Corson, with 162 Brownie Pack, Greenbank Church, in Braidburn Valley Park, *c.* 1947, when hay ricks and allotments were still very much in evidence. Those who can be identified are: *back row*, Jean Ramsay (second from the left); *second row*, Jean Dickerson (extreme left); *third row*, Hilda Gardner (second from the left); Winifred Galloway (second from the right); Marjorie Gibb (extreme right); *front row*, Elma Coghill (second from the right). *Courtesy of Miss Sheila Logie.*

❧ *Below right.* Preparations are being made for the Scout Fair at Slateford Public Hall in Inglis Green Road on Saturday 6 November 1948, 'Proceeds in Aid of 107th Edinburgh (Craiglockhart) Group Boy Scouts Building Fund'. The adults in the picture are: J. B. C. Brown, Scout Leader, on the left; Lorna Ramsay, Cub Leader, in the centre; and the Assistant Cub Leader, on the right. *Courtesy of Hamish Davidson.*

❧ *Below.* Staff-Sergeant Alex Segger of the 55th Boys' Brigade Company, St Matthew's Parish Church (now Morningside), on 27 June 1940, at a time when Douglas Sutherland was Captain. *Courtesy of Alex Segger.*

❧ *Above.* These two smartly dressed young men, Tommy Meek on the left, and Mike Imrie on the right, were doormen at the Plaza Ballroom in Morningside Road in 1933. The Plaza was the brainchild of Charles Jones who acquired the site on the corner of Falcon Avenue and Morningside Road in 1926 for the construction of Jones Motor House and the ballroom. *Courtesy of Elizabeth Casciani.*

❧ *Above left.* The Southern Light Opera Company performed *Merrie England* at the Open-Air Theatre in Braidburn Valley Park in June 1946. *Courtesy of Mrs G. Lowson.*

❧ *Left.* A Territorial Army picnic at Cramond, believed to be *c.* 1913. At the top right-hand corner of the picture is the horse and carriage which was driven by Hendry Baillie between Cramond and the railway stations at Davidson's Mains and Barnton.

Right. A large crowd has gathered in Waterloo Place, outside St Andrew's House, on 24 June 1953 for the ceremonial drive which took place in Edinburgh to mark the Coronation of Queen Elizabeth II at Westminster on 2 June. The State Drive began at St Giles Cathedral, proceeded down the Royal Mile to Holyrood Palace, up Regent Street, along Waterloo Place into Princes Street, and up the Mound, back to St Giles. In the photograph a section of the ceremonial parade is headed by a detachment of the Scots Guards, followed by the Royal Navy, while soldiers of the Black Watch line the route. *Photograph by Norward Inglis.*

Below. The combined military and pipe band of the Royal Scots, led by Band Sergeant Dan Sweeney, are at attention outside Bruntsfield School, in Montpelier, around the early spring of 1918. This is the 4th (Reserve) Battalion, a merger of the 4th and 3/9th (Highland) Battalion, which explains the wearing of the kilt by a Lowland regiment. While Bruntsfield School was requisitioned by the War Department during the First World War, the pupils were taught at Boroughmuir School which can just be seen in the top right-hand corner of the picture. *Malcolm Cant Collection.*

Below right. The pipe band of the North British Rubber Company in the 1920s appears to have just returned to base at Castle Mills. The position of the overhead gantry confirms that the photograph has been taken looking eastwards towards Gilmore Park. *Courtesy of Mrs Betty Styles, née McInnes.*

❧ *Left.* A bus stop is a wonderful vantage point from which to view the March of the 1000 Pipers along Princes Street on 18 August 1951. The total number of spectators was estimated at 500,000 which created immense problems of crowd control for Edinburgh City Police. The pipes and drums were led by Drum-Major John Seton, D.C.M., senior drum-major of the Scottish Pipe Band Association who had served with the Argyll and Sutherland Highlanders. The parade left Parliament Square at 1.15 p.m. and made its way, amid chaotic scenes, down Bank Street and the Mound for the grand march, sixteen abreast, along Princes Street to Torphichen Street. As the various bands were *en route* to Murrayfield to compete in the World Championship it was felt that they should be allowed to board buses for the last leg of the journey between Haymarket and Murrayfield. The pipers and drummers and clan standard bearers regrouped at Murrayfield before the Countess of Erroll, Hereditary Lord High Constable of Scotland, who took the salute. With such an outpouring of Scottish patriotism, it was inevitable that sections of the population would let their feelings be known – and how better to do it than with a huge white message painted on the Castle Rock – 'HOME RULE NOW' – the message, but not the sentiment, hurriedly removed by the authorities. *Photograph by Norward Inglis.*

❧ *Left and right below.* Scenes near Waverley Bridge on 26 May 2006 as the Royal Scots, formed in 1633, march for the last time before becoming part of the new Royal Regiment of Scotland. *Malcolm Cant Collection.*